CW00357765

A POCKET GUIDE
IN 101 MOMENTS, SONGS, PEOPLE AND PLACES

VIKKI REILLY

POLARIS
PUBLISHING

This edition first published in 2020 by

POLARIS PUBLISHING LTD
c/o Aberdein Considine
2nd Floor, Elder House
Multrees Walk
Edinburgh, EH1 3DX

Distributed by
Birlinn Limited

www.polarispublishing.com

Text copyright © Vikki Reilly, 2020

ISBN: 9781913538149
eBook ISBN: 9781913538064

The right of Vikki Reilly to be identified as the author of this work has been asserted by
her in accordance with the Copyright, Designs and Patents Act 1988.

All rights reserved. No part of this publication may be reproduced, stored or transmit-
ted in any form, or by any means electronic, mechanical, photocopying, recording or
otherwise, without the express written permission of the publisher.

Every effort has been made to trace copyright holders and obtain their permission for
the use of copyright material. The publisher apologises for any errors or omissions and
would be grateful if notified of any corrections that should be incorporated in future
reprints or editions of this book.

British Library Cataloguing-in-Publication Data
A catalogue record for this book is available on request from the British Library.

Designed and typeset by Polaris Publishing, Edinburgh

Printed and bound in Great Britain by Clays Ltd, Elcograf S.p.A.

Photos courtesy of:
Getty Images
Alamy

The things is, we're all really the same person.
We're just four parts of the one.
– Paul McCartney

For Mum, Dad and Jillian

INTRODUCTION

I can't remember the first time I heard The Beatles but I do remember rummaging through my mum and dad's small album collection – shelved in the cabinet under the defunct record player – and in amongst the Billy Connolly, Gilbert O'Sullivan and ABBA's greatest hits was *Sgt. Pepper's Lonely Hearts Club Band*. The cover disturbed me; the collage of serious faces, the drooping doll and the stern stone bust made more of an impression on me than the flowers and colourful uniforms. I also remember being dragged away, protesting, from watching *Yellow Submarine* to go to a family party, just as Fred and Ringo had got John, Paul and George on board to save Pepperland. Still, it wasn't until I started investigating The Beatles as a teenager that I realised how familiar their music already was to me. Thanks to my family's habit of playing the radio all day every Sunday, their songs had been with me all along.

In the summer holiday of 1992, when I was thirteen, a friend told me that her big brother had been playing her Beatles songs. I asked her to make me a mixtape, and she came back to me with a C90. I still have it, the tape sleeve covered in doodles of creepy crawlies and VW cars. The tracklist, which she didn't write down, was a bit haphazard; it was made up of *Sgt. Pepper* songs and a random collection of album tracks and some of the well-

On my way to becoming Ms Ringo Starr in the local church hall, the only place I was allowed to practice. You may recognise our band name on the drum.

known singles. It didn't matter to me; I didn't know any better. All I know is that I was hooked. My Beatles education continued with another mixtape made by a schoolfriend after I'd been evangelising about my new discovery. Raiding *her* parents' record collection, she gave me another strange, unlisted compilation – I still sometimes refer to Beatles songs by their first line rather than their title – from *Revolver*, *Beatles for Sale* and the *Love Songs* compilation. Everything crackled and skipped (it would be another couple of years before I heard the full second verse of 'I Don't Want to Spoil the Party'), but I loved it anyway.

I was never in a hurry to buy all the Beatles albums. I was happy to wait for Christmas and birthdays to add to my collection, which means that their music has always meant celebration to me. But like all teenage girls with their favourite bands, my friends, my sister and I fell hard for the Fabs, and we would go round shops and flea markets searching for posters, postcards, badges, stickers and old magazines to cut up (sacrilege!) to adorn our bedroom walls, coats, bags and school jotters. We subscribed to *The Beatles Book* monthly magazine, and I even started a Ringo Starr fan club, making pen pals across the world. We hunted down pirate videos and CDs of interviews and their Christmas records, we visited Liverpool, bought tickets for Beatles tribute acts, searched for the old Edinburgh home of John Lennon's aunt and uncle, read all the books, watched all the films, got excited by the *Anthology* project (new releases!) and always, always listened to the music. We got guitars, I got a drum kit, and we tried to perfect every harmony in every song. Sometimes we cracked them, sometimes we could only marvel at the way John, Paul and George's voices blended together. We busked the streets of Edinburgh, and my favourite memory is of singing in Rose Street when a guy and his girlfriend walked past us. 'Can you do "Helter Skelter"?' he asked sarcastically. Of course we could; we played the opening guitar line and screamed at the tops of our voices. He had the grace to walk back to us and give us a couple of quid.

What do I love most about The Beatles? Their audacity. Now, in 2020, The Beatles are part of our cultural fabric, beloved yet often taken for granted, seen as safe, and, if you're really cynical, just a billion-dollar industry. No. It still blows my mind after all this time as a fan, watching the *Anthology* documentary for the ninetieth time, to see just how explosive, how daring, how *new* they were. Four Northern lads so effortlessly themselves – honest, cheeky, irrepressible, boundlessly curious, funny, charming, challenging, unpredictable, utterly confident in their abilities – in a world that didn't know how much they needed them. Cosy? Never – not if you're really paying attention.

So, of course, there is the music, their joyous music. But it's their story too that is so unrivalled; it's a near perfect narrative. There are humble beginnings, global triumphs, heroes, villains, momentous shifts, drama, adventure, twists, turns and tragedy, and there are plenty of books out there that delve deep into their life and work. You should read them. (Have a look at the bibliography at the back where I've included some of my favourites.) What I hope to do here with *Beatles 101* is to give you a taster of their amazing story, to encourage you to join the legion of Beatlemaniacs. Dip your toe in here and then dive in – the water's FAB.

V.R.
Edinburgh, 2020

1

AND IN THE BEGINNING . . .

John Winston Lennon
Born: Wednesday, 9 October 1940

James Paul McCartney
Born: Thursday, 18 June 1942

George Harrison
Born: Thursday, 25 February 1943

Richard Starkey (Ringo Starr)
Born: Sunday, 7 July 1940

RINGO STARR was the first Beatle born and the last member to join the group, so he can claim to be both the oldest and youngest of the Fab Four. He was born to Elsie and Richard Starkey in the Dingle, one of Liverpool's roughest, most depressed areas, and just as he was born, the air raid sirens blared. At the time, there was no local shelter ready, so the family rushed into the coal hole to hide. According to Elsie, baby Ringo screamed all the way, and it wasn't until she had settled in that she realised she had been carrying her newborn upside down. She calmed him down and he slept through the rest of the air raid.

Ringo was plagued by illness throughout his childhood, suffering from peritonitis aged six, which resulted in a year's hospitalisation, including some time in a coma, and later, at thirteen, tuberculosis. This took two years to recover from, and he never returned to school.

His dad worked at a bakery and confectioners. He left the family when Ringo was only three years old. To keep house and home together Elsie took on work as a barmaid, working as many shifts as she could get. She later married Harry Graves, a painter and decorator from Romford, when Ringo was thirteen.

While no bombs were dropped on Liverpool the actual night JOHN LENNON was born, he too came into the world as the Luftwaffe were attacking the area. This probably accounts for John's parents giving him the middle name of Winston, after Churchill, in a gesture of momentary patriotism.

Alfred Lennon and Julia Stanley first met in 1927 in Liverpool's Sefton Park. He was dressed to impress the ladies – bowler-hatted and brandishing a cigarette holder – and when he spotted Julia, whom he'd seen before in a local dance hall, he decided to approach her. When Julia told him he looked silly, he told her she looked lovely and threw his hat into the pond. He was a cheeky, happy-go-lucky chancer, and she the rebellious, carefree daughter of a respectable family. Alfred was a waiter in the Merchant Navy, which meant he spent a lot of time away at sea, so they kept in touch through letters, meeting up when he was home on leave. Her family did not approve of the relationship. The couple married in 1938 on impulse, both returning to their respective family homes after the ceremony and their honeymoon at the cinema.

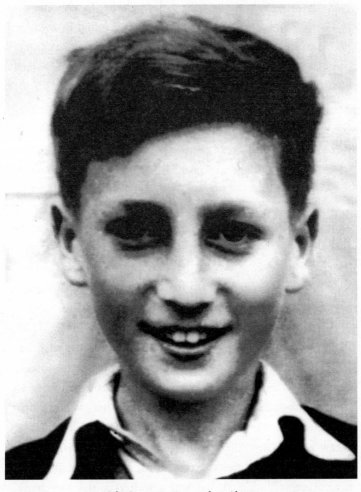

John Lennon as a young boy. *Alamy*

Baby John's home life was less than stable in his early years, and when Alfred and Julia finally split when John was four years old, Julia's big sister, Mary 'Mimi' Smith, was awarded custody. Mimi and her husband George, who had no children of their own, raised John. Sadly, George died when John was only fifteen. His mother

Julia began visiting him again when he was in his early teens, and bought him his first guitar when he was sixteen. She was knocked over by a car and killed two years later, leaving John devastated.

PAUL McCARTNEY's mum and dad settled down later than was usual at the time when they married in April 1941. Mary Mohin, thirty-two, had concentrated on her career as a nurse and midwife, and Jim McCartney, thirty-nine, was a cotton salesman and bandleader. When war broke out, Jim was deemed exempt

Young Paul McCartney and his brother, Michael. *Getty Images*

from service due to a hearing impairment. Instead, he volunteered to be a home front fireman, which meant he was not present for Paul's birth at Walton hospital.

Paul's younger brother, Michael, was born in 1944, and though Mary now had two young children she carried on working. As Liverpool's cotton industry fell on hard times she became the main breadwinner. The McCartney family moved around frequently during Paul's childhood due to his mother's job taking her to different areas of Liverpool. In 1956, when Paul was fourteen, Mary died after breast cancer surgery, leaving Jim to bring up his teenage boys.

GEORGE HARRISON had the least dramatic birth and early childhood of The Beatles. He was born the youngest of four children to shop assistant Louise and Harold Harrison. George's father had started out in the Merchant Navy, lying about his age to be accepted, before becoming a bus driver. His mum was a music fan who used to sing at home, sometimes so loudly she rattled the windows, and his dad bought him his first guitar in 1956. His independent outlook started from a young age: he would happily go on errands, alone, for his family as a boy, and he insisted on walking to school himself when he started attending Dovedale Primary School.

2

AND THE FABS BEGIN TO PLAY

In reminiscences about his earliest musical memories John often contradicts himself. So, while it is pretty certain that the first instrument he taught himself to play was the harmonica, there are different stories about who it was that introduced him to the instrument. After her husband's death Mimi rented out rooms to local university students, and it is most likely that one of the lodgers gave John his first harmonica.

In John's early teens he re-established a relationship with his mother, who lived with a new partner in a nearby neighbourhood. It was Julia who taught John how to play the banjo, first teaching him the Fats Domino classic 'Ain't That A Shame'.

Though Paul's dad had left his band days behind him, he would often play the piano and sing standards such as 'Stairway To Paradise' and 'Lullaby Of Leaves' in the evening and at family parties. Paul would lie on the carpet, taking it all in. His dad encouraged him to take piano lessons, but Paul wasn't interested in the discipline of learning scales and reading music, preferring to teach himself by ear and instinct.

When Paul turned thirteen, his dad bought him a trumpet. Paul was enthusiastic, teaching himself 'When The Saints Go Marching In', but he soon realised he couldn't sing with a trumpet in his mouth, so he traded it in for a guitar. In the beginning, he couldn't get anything out of the instrument. The guitar strings had to be adjusted because he was left-handed. He practised obsessively, sometimes singing harmonies with his brother Michael, but most of the time with his friend Ian James, an avid record collector who fortunately knew more chords than Paul.

George grew up in a home with a gregarious, supportive mother who loved to play the radio all day; he was always surrounded by the latest, and sometimes the most esoteric, sounds. His first musical memory that stuck was listening to one of country music's first stars, Jimmie Rodgers.

George as a child playing guitar. *Alamy*

Ringo (second from left) with Rory Storm and
the Hurricanes at Butlin's Holiday Camp. *Alamy*

When George was twelve he was hospitalised with nephritis, a kidney disorder. At school he had started to draw guitars in his exercise books rather than pay attention to his teachers, so while in the hospital, he asked his mother for a guitar. She and George's dad scrimped and saved to grant him his wish, and once back home he would practise into the early hours until his fingers bled. Louise, ever encouraging, would stay up with him, cheering him on and bringing him cups of tea.

Like George, Ringo's first musical memory came from country music – hearing Gene Autry singing 'South Of The Border'.

When in hospital recovering from pleurisy and tuberculosis, his ward was visited by a music teacher, who would bring percussion instruments for the patients. Ringo would only join in if he was given the drum.

Healthy again, Ringo managed to get a thirty-bob bass drum, and he made a snare drum out of a biscuit tin and metal wires. In 1956, for Christmas, his stepdad Harry gave Ringo a drum kit. After much enthusiastic practising in the house – and a lot of complaining from the neighbours – Ringo realised he would have to join a band to be able to play.

3

FROM 'HEARTBREAK HOTEL' TO THE PEEL STREET LABOUR CLUB

Hearing Elvis Presley's 'Heartbreak Hotel' for the first time changed everything. Then Little Richard, Gene Vincent, Carl Perkins, Eddie Cochran . . . John switched his allegiance from the banjo to the guitar – though he used banjo tuning and played banjo chords – and decided to start a band.

In the UK at the time, the other big music craze was skiffle, spearheaded by Glasgow-born Lonnie Donegan who had massive chart success with songs such as Leadbelly's 'Rock Island Line' and 'Cumberland Gap'. With its appealing DIY ethic and improvised instruments, including the tea chest bass, washboard and kazoo, skiffle was popping up everywhere, including Liverpool. John gathered together a gang of friends from Quarry Bank High School to form a band, and each was given a role to play. John was the frontman and leader. They called themselves The Quarrymen after their school. Though the line-up often changed, the original line-up consisted of John on guitar and lead vocals, his best friend Pete Shotton on washboard, Eric Griffiths also on guitar, Bill Smith on the tea chest bass and Colin Hanton on drums.

Their first official engagement was an audition for Carroll Levis, 'Mr Star-Maker', who ran talent contests across the country to find acts for television variety shows. The Quarrymen failed to qualify.

Paul's first public performance was with his brother, at the Butlin's holiday camp in Filey Bay, Yorkshire. They sang 'Bye Bye Love' by The Everly Brothers, Michael in a sling as he had broken his arm at scout camp just before the holiday. After the duet, Paul treated the audience to his Little Richard routine. They didn't progress to the next round.

George, ever the independently minded individual he'd been since childhood, managed to get himself a booking before he even had a band. So, due to play the British Legion club in Speke, he convinced his brother Pete, his friend Arthur Kelly and another local boy, Alan Williams, to join him on stage. They called themselves The Rebels, and played to about half a dozen people.

Ringo's health problems meant he had trouble getting and holding on to jobs once he had left school. Finally, he managed to get himself an engineer's apprenticeship at H. Hunt & Sons. There he joined the work band, the Eddie Clayton Skiffle Group. Guitarist and vocalist Eddie Clayton was really Eddie Miles (and Ringo's neighbour), and they were joined by Roy Trafford on tea chest bass, John Dougherty on washboard and Frank Walsh also on guitar. They played during lunch breaks in the staff canteen and made their official debut at the Peel Street Labour Club where they soon took up a residency. They played The Cavern multiple times too, before disbanding when Eddie decided to settle down and get married.

4

ALL THESE PLACES HAD THEIR MOMENTS

WHEN JOHN MET PAUL

*I just thought, 'Well, he looks good, he's singing well and
he seems like a great lead singer to me.' Of course, he
had his glasses off, so he really looked suave.*
– Paul McCartney

Saturday, 6 July 1957
Woolton Garden Fete, St Peter's Church

The ingredients were just right. It was the season for summer galas,
parties and fetes. Both skiffle and rock 'n' roll were mainstays in
the charts. Planning committees across the UK were allowing the
kids their spots to shine in front of their communities in between
the usual fancy dress contests, vegetable-growing competitions
and raffles. St Peter's Church in Woolton was no different,
booking The Quarrymen for three slots, two in the afternoon and
one in the evening.

Ivan Vaughan, a friend of John's since childhood and sometime
member of The Quarrymen, had a pal over in Allerton he'd
befriended at the Liverpool Institute, Vaughan's high school. He
was as obsessed with rock 'n' roll as John and could play a bit too.
He felt they might have a lot in common.

Paul was keen to go to the fete with Ivan. It was a hot, sunny day, and there might be some good-looking girls to chat up. He donned his favourite white sports jacket and drainpipe trousers and cycled over to Woolton.

The Liverpool Police Dogs Display was over, and The Quarrymen were on stage when Ivan and Paul arrived. Right away, Paul noticed the singer. He had presence and attitude, despite his shortcomings in technique, and he was singing a song – 'Come Go With Me' by the American doo-wop group The Del-Vikings – that was impressively obscure. Not only that, but he was singing his own lyrics, changing it from a romantic love song into something bluesier. Paul appreciated his cheek.

Later, in the scout hut before The Quarrymen's evening slot, a few beers were taken, and Ivan finally introduced Paul to John. Paul, slightly intimidated, being two years younger, was handed a guitar. There was pointing and laughing when he first retuned the guitar away from John's banjo chords, and flipped it upside down to accommodate his left-handedness. But then he launched into a word-perfect, smoothly played rendition of Eddie Cochran's 'Twenty Flight Rock', another relatively obscure song at the time. He followed this up with Gene Vincent's 'Be-Bop-A-Lula', one of John's favourites. Confidence rising, Paul switched to the piano and gave a screaming rendition of Little Richard's 'Long Tall Sally', showing as much front as Lennon had earlier.

John now had a decision to make. Paul was obviously the better player and he'd really strengthen his band, but The Quarrymen was *his* band. Would Paul's talent dilute his place as leader?

Memories of John asking Paul to join the band differ from person to person, but what seems most likely is that Pete Shotton bumped into Paul on his bicycle days later and passed on the message that John wanted him to join. Paul agreed and cycled away.

However, Paul couldn't play with The Quarrymen at their next gig – their first in the Cavern Club – as he was at scout camp. He joined them at their next gig at the Conservative Club in New Clubmoor Hall. Nerves got the better of him, and he flubbed his guitar solo during 'Guitar Boogie'. He didn't play another solo for The Quarrymen. What might've been if Paul had succeeded?

5

GEORGE JOINS THE BAND

I remember being very impressed with John's big thick sideboards and trendy Teddy boy clothes . . . I was never intimidated by him. Whenever he had a go at me I just gave him a little bit of his own right back.
– George Harrison

The Quarrymen were still on the hunt for a lead guitarist. Paul suggested his friend George; he thought he'd be a great addition to the band.

George and Paul lived one bus stop away from each other and had become friends travelling in to the Liverpool Institute, talking about music, recommending records to each other and, later, playing together in the institute where George taught Paul new chords. George was younger than Paul, but self-assured and an obvious rock 'n' roll fan. He wore coloured shirts, drainpipes and a huge quiff – much to the consternation of his teachers.

John had to be convinced. He had already allowed the baby-faced fifteen-year-old McCartney into his band, and George looked even younger – not ideal for a Ted looking for street cred.

Still, one evening the three of them were on the top deck of an otherwise empty bus, and George, as usual, had his guitar with him. Paul encouraged him to play the instrumental 'Raunchy', a lesser known record from Sam Phillips' Sun Records by Bill Justis. George's rendition was note-perfect, John was impressed, and George was in.

6

JOHN AND PAUL START WRITING

Every time I approach a song, there's no rules.
Sometimes the music comes first, sometimes the
words – and if you're lucky, it all comes together.
– Paul McCartney

John and Paul started to spend time together away from The Quarrymen to find out more about each other's musical interests. One of the first songs they learned to play together was Buddy Holly's 'That'll Be The Day' with Paul showing John guitar chords. Both also found out that, like Holly, they had each written songs of their own. When John was first teaching himself the guitar he created 'Calypso Rock' and later 'Hello Little Girl', while Paul had written the Sinatra-style 'I Call It Suicide' (inspired by his dad's piano composition 'Walking In The Park With Eloise' and later recorded by Paul in 1974 with Wings and Chet Atkins, under the name of The Country Hams), a dance band number, 'When I'm Sixty Four' and, on guitar, 'I Lost My Little Girl'.

The first songs they wrote together were called 'Too Bad About Sorrows' and 'Because I Know You Love Me', though neither were shown to The Quarrymen; they remained uncompleted and unrecorded. This was the case with other early songs, such as 'I've Been Thinking You Love Me', 'If Tomorrow Ever Comes' and 'Years Roll Along'. At this time, though, they did write 'Love Me

16

Buddy Holly, a huge influence on The Beatles. *Alamy*

Do' and 'I Call Your Name', which would make their way into The Beatles' repertoire later.

As Paul's dad didn't approve of his new friendship with John, these songwriting sessions usually took place during the day when Jim was at work. Skipping school and art college, they would sit face to face, smoking, drinking tea, strumming their guitars, seeing what they could create. Quickly, they established a rule that if they couldn't remember a song they had written the day before, it would be scrapped: if it wasn't memorable to them, it wouldn't be memorable to an audience. However, in their live sets, they stuck to covers for the moment.

7

THE FIFTH BEATLE

STUART SUTCLIFFE

Miles ahead of everybody.
– Klaus Voormann

Stuart Fergusson Victor Sutcliffe was born in Edinburgh on 23 June 1940, to senior civil servant Charles Sutcliffe and schoolteacher Millie. The family moved to Liverpool in 1943 to help with the war effort, and Charles became a ship's engineer, which meant he spent most of Stuart's childhood at sea. There were two younger sisters, three older half-brothers and one older half-sister from his father's first marriage.

Stuart was introduced to John at art school by a mutual friend, Bill Harry (who would later found *Mersey Beat* magazine), at the students' regular hangout, Ye Cracke pub. At first glance, John and Stuart's friendship seemed an unlikely one: Stuart was introverted, sensitive and dedicated to his studies, while John was loudmouthed, tough and did as little as was possible in class. Each, though, respected the other's talent, and saw more in each other than was superficially apparent.

In 1959, one of Stuart's artworks, *Summer Painting*, was chosen to be exhibited in the prestigious John Moores Liverpool Exhibition alongside works from artists such as Henry Moore and Barbara Hepworth. His painting sold for £65 (though there are varying accounts of how much money Stuart actually received in the end) – a huge sum for an art student, and he was persuaded by John and Paul to buy a Hofner President bass guitar and join the band.

Stuart was a rock 'n' roll fan and keen to be involved, particularly as he had an artistic sensibility and a curiosity about image. He had taken piano lessons as a youngster and his dad had given him a guitar, but the bass was completely new to him. His playing has been criticised over the years, but it was adequate for a hard-playing rock 'n' roll band kicking off their career, and he had a seriously cool, brooding presence on stage. When he sang Elvis Presley's 'Love Me Tender', the audience, particularly the girls, loved it. And once Stuart joined the band, encouraging opportunities came knocking . . .

(L-R) George, John, Paul & Stuart Sutcliffe, in an iconic
Hamburg picture, taken by Astrid Kircherr. *Alamy*

8

FROM THE QUARRYMEN TO THE BEATLES

It was beat and beetles, and when you said it, people thought of crawly things, and when you read it, it was beat music.
– John Lennon

The last hurrah for The Quarrymen was their first recording, a shellac demo disc made in 1958 with John singing lead on both sides. The A-side was a cover of Buddy Holly's 'That'll Be The Day', the B-side a McCartney-Harrison composition called 'In Spite Of All The Danger'. After this recording, due to too many squabbles, the line-up of the band dwindled to core members John, Paul and George.

The band name was dropped, and when another chance to audition for Carroll Levis came up, the three performed as Johnny and the Moondogs. Only George and Paul brought their guitars on this occasion, and John sang in between them both, hamming it up with a hand on each of their shoulders. Despite this, they passed the audition, but unfortunately missed their spot in the final round in Manchester's Hippodrome Theatre. It was late in the evening and they didn't want to miss the last train back to Liverpool.

They briefly called themselves Japage 3 (from **J**ohn **a**nd **Pa**ul and **Ge**orge) to play at a Harrison family wedding and another gig in Runcorn, and once performed as The Rainbows while wearing

(L-R) John, George, Paul & Pete Best in their first professional photo shoot. *Getty Images*

different coloured shirts. And on a visit to Paul's cousins, John and Paul played in their Fox and Hounds pub in Caversham as The Nerk Twins.

There has always been uncertainty as to when the band finally became The Beatles. John famously mythologised the name as coming from a man on a 'flaming pie' he saw in a vision, and the Marlon Brando biker film *The Wild One* has often (erroneously) been cited as the influence due to Lee Marvin's character Chino's remark about the 'beetles'. The name most likely came from John and Stuart Sutcliffe – both Buddy Holly and The Crickets fans – bandying about possibilities while exploring puns and thinking about the double meaning behind 'The Crickets'. It is claimed that Stuart came up with The Beatals, and John changed it to The Beatles. (Paul recalls both telling him of the name they'd dreamt up the next day.)

The name change came just as the band had another audition, this time for impresario Larry Parnes, famous for his stable of rock 'n' roll solo acts, including Tommy Steele, Billy Fury and Marty Wilde. They were told that a band should have a long name and so Long John and The Silver Beatles was suggested. This was shortened to The Silver Beatles for the audition to go on tour supporting one of Parnes' star acts, Billy Fury. They didn't pass that audition, but The Silver Beatles were employed to back another of Parnes' singers, Johnny Gentle, on a two-week tour of Scotland.

Back from the tour, they had gigs with variations on the name, trying out The Silver Beats and The Silver Beetles, finally settling on The Beatles in August 1960.

9

THE FIFTH BEATLE

PETE BEST

We were at our best when we were playing in the dance halls of Liverpool and Hamburg. The world never saw that.
— Pete Best

As the rock 'n' roll scene in Liverpool grew, so too did the number of venues where bands could play. One of the key Liverpool venues was the Casbah, run by the indomitable Mona Best in the cellar of her house. Mona decided to convert the space into a coffee bar after noticing her eldest son's growing love for rock 'n' roll. In exchange for a residency there, John, Paul and George painted the cellar before its opening. But it wasn't until an offer came to play in Hamburg, in 1960, under the condition that they become a five-piece band with a drummer, that they got in touch with that son, Pete.

Randolph Peter Scanland was born in Madras (now Chennai), India, on 24 November 1941. Mona and his father, marine engineer Donald Peter Scanland (who later died during the Second World War), were not married. Mona was training to become a doctor for the Red Cross when she met Johnny Best, a boxing promoter from Liverpool stationed in India as a physical training instructor. They married and had a child, Rory, before moving back to Liverpool in 1945.

Pete was a quiet child, and Mona was keen to bring him out

of his shell. He was a talented rugby player, did well at school, and was on track to go to college to become a PE teacher, but he suddenly lost interest in his studies. After the Casbah had opened and she noticed Pete fiddling about with a drum kit a band had left behind, Mona bought him a kit of his own and encouraged him to join a band. He formed The Black Jacks with local players Chas Newby, Bill Barlow and Ken Brown, an ex-member of The Quarrymen. Mona gave them a residency in her coffee bar once The Beatles' stint came to an end after a pay dispute.

Pete was hugely popular with female fans owing to his good looks, and he found himself increasingly attracted to life as a musician. Unfortunately, the other members of The Black Jacks were losing interest, looking to settle down. It was at this time that Pete received the phone call from Paul asking him to join The Beatles for the trip to Hamburg. He auditioned for them – though it was really only a formality – at the Wyvern Social Club and duly set off for Germany with John, Paul, George and Stuart on 16 August 1960.

After Pete Best was replaced by Ringo, Pete joined Lee Curtis and the All-Stars, later becoming Pete Best and the All-Stars to capitalise on his popularity with The Beatles. The band were signed to Decca and released a single, 'I'm Gonna Knock On Your Door'. The song didn't chart. Pete continued to play throughout the sixties, as well as working in a bakery, but grew increasingly downhearted at his missed opportunity and even attempted suicide by gassing himself in 1965. Eventually he gave up on the music industry and worked contentedly as a civil servant in Liverpool for over twenty years. He married and had two daughters and, as the decades passed, became more comfortable in giving interviews about his time with The Beatles, taking part in conventions, and touring with his new band, The Pete Best Band.

10

ALL THESE PLACES HAD THEIR MOMENTS

HAMBURG

*We got better and got more confidence. We couldn't help
it, with all the experience, playing all night long.*
– John Lennon

Allan Williams was a Liverpool entrepreneur as enamoured with
the rising music scene as the young Liverpudlians who were
forming bands. He opened the Jacaranda club in 1958 with an
eclectic booking policy. One of his favoured bands was Harold
'Lord Woodbine' Phillips' All-Steel Caribbean Band. They told
him that Hamburg had a buzzing club scene too and that the club
owners were always looking out for bands. Sensing an opportunity,
he made a recording featuring one of the top Liverpool beat groups,
Cass and the Casanovas, and took it to Hamburg. There, he met
Bruno Koschmider, manager of the Kaiserkeller, and talked up how
the Liverpool scene was far more exciting than anywhere else in the
UK. Unfortunately, when he played Bruno his tape, the recording
was faulty, and he left Hamburg unable to back up his claims.

Then, a little bit of luck. In the summer of 1960, Williams
found himself in Soho's 2i's coffee bar, the hub of London's beat
scene. By a happy coincidence Bruno Koschmider was in the
audience, checking out bands. In yet another happy coincidence,
Liverpool's Derry and the Seniors were on the bill and smashed
their set, blowing away the local bands, just as Williams had tried

to convince Koschmider earlier. Williams secured a residency for Derry and the Seniors at the Kaiserkeller, and told Koschmider he had more bands he could send over.

The German entrepreneur also ran another club, the Indra, which he had decided to transform from a transvestite cabaret bar into a rock 'n' roll venue. He asked Williams for a five-piece band, and the latter asked Rory Storm and the Hurricanes, Cass and the Casanovas and Gerry and the Pacemakers if they wanted to go over to Hamburg. They all said no. As a last resort he asked The Beatles – with Pete Best on drums they were now a five-piece – and they agreed. They all set off in a Morris J2 minibus, with their equipment and a tub of scones baked by George's mum.

Liverpool had a reputation for being a tough city, but it was a playground in comparison to Hamburg and its St Pauli district in particular. The Reeperbahn teemed with pickpockets, prostitutes, pimps, strippers, sailors on leave and war-scarred ex-soldiers, who frequented the strip joints and bars. On arrival, The Beatles were shown to their digs – the backrooms of Koschmider's Bambi cinema. One window, one electric light, no heating, no furniture except a couple of camp beds and a small couch, and a ceiling so low the band had to duck their heads. Their toilet was shared with the cinema's customers. Assured that their accommodation was only temporary – it wasn't – the band settled in, taking advantage of all the sensual delights the city had to offer (George lost his virginity on one of the camp beds with the rest of the band cheering him on), and got to work.

For around £15 a week, The Beatles had to play sets of four and a half hours Tuesday to Friday, and sets of six hours on Saturday and Sunday, with a day off on Monday. The band had a repertoire that could stretch to two hours at most, so they decided that rather than repeating themselves every night they would keep their shows fresh and exciting for the audience and themselves. They quickly expanded their set list, spinning out popular songs such as Ray Charles' 'What I'd Say' (it could last a good forty minutes) and tackling the entire catalogue of their favourite artists, Little Richard, Chuck Berry and Buddy Holly. They introduced jazz standards and show tunes – 'Summertime', 'Moonglow', 'Over The Rainbow', 'Bésame Mucho' – to their set as well as early Motown and girl group material – 'To Know Him Is To Love Him', 'Money (That's What I Want)' – to complement their rock 'n' roll, bluesy and country numbers. Koschmider would loudly encourage them to 'Mach schau!' – put on a show – and The Beatles would respond by leaping about, stomping along to the music, acting up on stage and goading the audience. The punters lapped it up, sending drinks and requests to the stage in a raucous call-and-response. And if they got too rowdy, the waiters were always on hand with their fists or, on some occasions, tear gas, to calm things down . . .

So successful were The Beatles at the Indra that, due to noise complaints, they were moved to the bigger Kaiserkeller after Derry and the Seniors had finished their residency, and their contract was extended. Koschmider also brought in Rory Storm and the Hurricanes – they had finished their Butlin's summer season – to share playing duties.

Rory Storm and the Hurricanes, long the top Liverpool band, were astounded by the change in The Beatles. They hadn't been considered serious contenders back in Liverpool. Both bands started a friendly rivalry on stage, trying to outdo each other in getting the best audience reaction. Off stage, they would often socialise together, in particular with Rory Storm's drummer, Ringo Starr, who would sit in for Pete Best when he was ill or unable to perform.

The Beatles also struck up a friendship with a group of young Germans who had become regular visitors to their shows. Klaus Voormann, Astrid Kirchherr and Jürgen Vollmer were cool art students inspired by existentialism as well as lovers of rock 'n' roll. Both they and The Beatles influenced each other's music, fashion and art, and Kirchherr, herself a talented photographer, fell in love with Stuart Sutcliffe. She took numerous photographs of The Beatles during their first trip, now iconic and among the best pictures of the band. Voormann went on to play bass with Manfred Mann as well as design the cover art for The Beatles' *Revolver* album, and Vollmer later gave the band their moptop haircut.

But back in 1960, The Beatles had come to the attention of Peter Eckhorn, owner of the biggest live venue in Hamburg, the Top Ten Club. He approached them about a residency there, which The Beatles were keen to take up, particularly as their relationship with Koschmider was becoming increasingly strained. Just then, George, still only seventeen, was busted for being underage. At that time, Hamburg imposed a night-time curfew for the under-18s, so George was sent home.

Paul and Pete went to the Bambi to pick up their clothes and equipment to take to the Top Ten, and as a cheeky gesture to Koschmider, decided to stick condoms on the walls of their squalid digs and set them alight. Although the worst that happened was that they left greasy marks on the walls, Koschmider had them arrested for arson. He later dropped the charges, but Paul and Pete were sent home. John soon followed, dejected. Sutcliffe stayed on a little longer, reluctant to leave Kirchherr.

In April 1961, with George now eighteen, The Beatles headed back to Hamburg and straight to the Top Ten Club. They stayed in better digs this time, with Top Ten headliner Tony Sheridan – though

Sutcliffe moved in with Kirchherr – and had to play seven-hour sets on weekdays and eight-hour sets on weekends. No days off. It was on this trip that the group were introduced to amphetamines, particularly Preludin ('prellies'), to keep up with the relentless pace.

Hamburg was the city at the centre of the German recording business, and talent spotters would often drop in to the Top Ten Club. On a recommendation from a friend, Bert Kaempfert, an orchestra leader and music producer for Polydor Records, took in a Beatles performance and promptly signed them up for a recording session with Tony Sheridan. They backed him on his popular songs, 'My Bonnie (Lies Over the Ocean)', 'When The Saints Go Marching In', 'Nobody's Child', 'Take Out Some Insurance On Me, Baby' and Sheridan's self-penned 'Why (Can't You Love Me Again)'. They recorded two songs without Sheridan: 'Ain't She Sweet' and a Lennon-Harrison instrumental 'Cry For A Shadow'. Sutcliffe attended the sessions but he didn't play on any of the tracks.

He was playing fewer gigs with The Beatles this time round and had applied to the art school in Hamburg, taking classes with Edinburgh-born artist and sculptor Eduardo Paolozzi. Sutcliffe decided to leave the band, and played an emotional final gig with them before John, Paul, George and Pete returned to Liverpool without him. Paul, though reluctant at first, became the group's bass player.

In April 1962, on the cusp of signing a recording contract with Parlophone, The Beatles returned to Hamburg for a residency in the new Star Club, where they shared the bill with one of their musical heroes, Gene Vincent, for two weeks. Astrid Kirchherr flew to Liverpool, and the band met her at the airport. It was there that she told them the tragic news that Sutcliffe, who had been

Mad-eyed Beatles showing off their Preludin in Hamburg. *Getty Images*

suffering from debilitating headaches, had collapsed and died with a brain aneurysm. The band, especially John, were shattered.

They returned to the Star Club in November to support Little Richard, this time with their new drummer, Ringo. 'Love Me Do' had just been released, and the band were reluctant to leave the UK, worried that their absence might hamper the single's progress up the chart, but their manager Brian Epstein was adamant: they should honour their agreements. Fortunately, 'Love Me Do' went on to surpass Parlophone's expectations, but there were grumbles when they had to travel back to Hamburg in late December 1962 for their final stint at the Star Club. During this last trip, the band were recorded on a reel-to-reel deck by Ted 'King Size' Taylor of The Dominoes, and this was later released as an album in 1977 as *Live! At The Star Club*, an amazing document of a band rough, ready, off the leash and on the cusp of stardom.

11

†††

ALL THESE PLACES HAD THEIR MOMENTS

THE CAVERN

If the Beatles had only been playing church halls
in Maghull, would anyone have taken any notice?
– Alan Sytner

Of all the Liverpool venues associated with the rise of The Beatles, none is more iconic than the cellar bar on Mathew Street – the centre of the city's fruit and veg market – the Cavern Club.

The venue was opened in 1957 by Alan Sytner, inspired by the jazz clubs he'd visited in Paris on his summer holidays as a teenager. He made the decision early on to have an unlicensed bar as he wanted the venue to be known for its music. In the beginning, the music policy did not include rock 'n' roll, and when The Beatles (still The Quarrymen at this point), played their first gig there in August, Sytner sent up an angry note to them on stage after John sang 'Hound Dog' and 'Blue Suede Shoes'.

When Sytner moved to London to work for the National Jazz Federation, he sold the club to Ray McFall, who worked for the club's accountants. There was no official announcement that the music policy was changing, but Ray started to book more rock 'n' roll acts and he introduced lunchtime sessions, which became much loved by Liverpool's young workers.

After The Beatles' transformative first trip to Hamburg, the Liverpool audiences grew in size and devotion. The band played

31

their first Cavern lunchtime session on 9 February 1961 and went on to dominate that spot, playing it over 150 times between February 1961 and February 1963. They played many night-time sessions too, chalking up nearly 300 gigs in the venue altogether.

They made the place their own, creating an intimate, unique relationship with their audience. It was a unique space anyway, with its signature aroma of disinfectant, damp, rotting fruit, smoke, cooking and bodies. Sweat would run down the walls, the electrics would blow, and The Beatles would take it all in their stride, playing dirty rock 'n' roll, cracking jokes, and parodying adverts and jingles.

They played their last gig at the Cavern on Saturday, 3 August 1963, selling out the tickets in half an hour. By this time Beatlemania had hit.

12

THE FIFTH BEATLE

BRIAN EPSTEIN

*These boys are going to explode. I am completely
confident that one day they will be bigger than Elvis Presley.*
– Brian Epstein

The Epsteins arrived in Liverpool in 1896, having escaped the Russian pogroms, and by the time Brian Samuel Epstein was born there, on 19 September 1934, they'd built up a successful furniture retail business.

Despite his family's wealth and support, Brian had a troubled childhood, bouncing from boarding school to boarding school across the country. Obsessed with the theatre, he paid scant attention to his lessons and dreamt only of performance, of becoming an actor or a costume designer. He was expelled from one school for drawing pictures of showgirls. He had trouble fitting in, and was constantly restless, aware of subtle and not so subtle anti-Semitism and unable to deal with his burgeoning homosexuality.

He was desperate to find a community in which he could be himself. He certainly did not want to join the family business, but with his options running out, he started working for one of his dad's furniture stores and discovered that he was a natural salesman. He had a good rapport with customers and prided himself on fair deals for both the customer and the business.

He was then called up for National Service and stationed in London where he was delighted to indulge in his love of culture. His troubles followed him, though, and he was given an honourable discharge on medical grounds.

Back in Liverpool, he moved from selling furniture to selling music. He was given his own store to run, where he sold instruments, sheet music, record players and records. He was hugely successful and built excellent relationships with key record companies down in London. Still, he couldn't settle, and surprised his parents by auditioning and getting accepted into RADA. He moved back to London, but once again, his time there was an unhappy one.

He enjoyed the classes, but his fellow students' narcissism left him feeling frustrated and isolated. His compulsion to put himself in dangerous sexual situations – in a time when homosexuality was illegal – resulted in him being arrested, charged and found guilty of importuning by the military police. He avoided a custodial sentence by agreeing to psychiatry sessions, during which he confessed his homosexuality.

Brian Epstein looks out at the sell-out crowd at the Beatles gig in Shea Stadium. *Alamy*

Back he came to Liverpool, and this time he was determined to make his mark. The family gave him a three-storey city-centre store (the North End Road Music Store, or NEMS) to manage, and he vowed to make it the best record shop in the north of England. Using his connections, he persuaded entertainer Anthony Newley to open it and successfully negotiated a generous discount from EMI. In the first month, his turnover exceeded the annual turnover of his previous shop. He started a record review column in the new *Mersey Beat* magazine, edited by Bill Harry, a friend of John. Epstein had found his feet at last.

On 28 October 1961, Raymond Jones, a regular at Beatles gigs at the Cavern, went into the NEMS store to ask for 'My Bonnie', the single The Beatles had cut with Tony Sheridan in Hamburg. It wasn't in stock, but Epstein investigated ordering the import. He had a policy of ordering three copies of everything: one for the customer and two for the shelves. Over the next few days, there were more requests for the same record.

On 9 November, Epstein visited the Cavern to see The Beatles. Afterwards, he told his assistant Alistair Taylor that he wanted to manage them, though he went to more shows to make sure. He was particularly taken with their personality on stage; they were natural, fun and, most important, authentic.

He got to work right away, getting in touch with EMI's marketing manager Ron White, who promised he would get his four leading A&R men – of which one was future producer George Martin – to listen to an audition tape. He also contacted Sidney Beecher-Stevens, Decca's sales manager, who put in motion the label's standard audition agreement. In less than a month, Mike Smith, an A&R assistant, was dispatched from London to the Cavern where it was agreed that The Beatles would come down to the Decca studios for an official audition.

13

THE DECCA AUDITON

Mr Epstein, we don't like your boys' sound . . .

The band travelled to London, battling snow, ice and fog to make it in time for their 10 a.m. slot at Decca's West Hampstead studios on New Year's Day, 1962. They had decided on a setlist of fifteen songs to highlight the diversity of their influences and versatility, including three Lennon-McCartney originals – 'Like Dreamers Do', 'Hello Little Girl' and 'Love Of The Loved' – for the climax. Although Paul and John had been writing songs sporadically after they had met, they very rarely included them in their sets before Epstein started managing them. He was convinced that this writing partnership was what set them apart.

Money (That's What I Want)
The Sheik Of Araby
Memphis, Tennessee
Three Cool Cats
Sure To Fall
September In The Rain
Take Good Care Of My Baby
Till There Was You
Crying, Waiting, Hoping
To Know Her Is To Love Her
Bésame Mucho

Searchin'
Like Dreamers Do
Hello Little Girl
Love Of The Loved

Cold, tired, nervous, a little hungover from New Years' Eve celebrations, and completely unfamiliar with a studio environment, The Beatles gave a lacklustre, uptight performance. They were rejected, with Dick Rowe, Decca's Head of A&R, making the now infamous assertion that 'groups of guitarists are on their way out'.

14

THE FIFTH BEATLE

GEORGE MARTIN

He'd dealt with navigators and pilots.
He could deal with us when we got out of line.
– Paul McCartney

George Henry Martin was born in Holloway, London, on 3 March 1926, the youngest child of carpenter Henry Martin and his wife Bertha. His parents were not musical, but there was a piano in the family home, and George took his first lessons when he was eight years old. Later, when he was evacuated to Bromley with his family as a teenager, he formed his own dance band, playing in local clubs and schools.

He left school with distinctions in French and maths and dreamt of designing aircraft. Instead, with the war on, he volunteered for the Fleet Air Arm in the Royal Navy, first being posted to Jamaica and then to New York where he enjoyed the jazz scene. He was promoted to officer, ironed out his accent, and continued to play piano.

After leaving the Navy, he auditioned for the Guildhall School of Music and was accepted. He studied there – playing piano and oboe – for three years, though he did not achieve a final examination pass. (His oboe teacher was one Margaret Eliot, mother of Jane Asher, who would later have a relationship with Paul throughout the sixties.)

After Guildhall, Martin took a clerical job in the BBC's music library and continued to play the oboe in gigs across London. He was then offered the job of A&R assistant at Parlophone, an EMI subsidiary known for its more eclectic signings. By 1954, he headed up the label.

Here, he widened his musical palette working with every kind of music from around the world. He had successes in jazz with Humphrey Lyttelton (achieving his first number one hit,

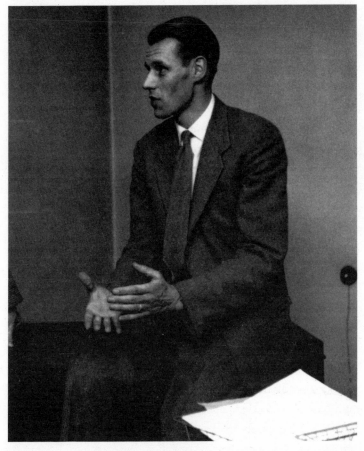

A dapper, dashing George Martin. *Alamy*

'You're Driving Me Crazy', with the novelty trad jazz outfit The Temperance Seven), in children's music with 'Nellie The Elephant', in skiffle with The Vipers, in ballads with Matt Monro, and, most famously, in comedy with The Goons, Beyond the Fringe, Rolf Harris and Bernard Cribbins.

When Martin first heard The Beatles, he was far from impressed. By this time, Brian Epstein had visited Robert Boast at HMV (also owned by EMI), who transferred the Decca audition tape to vinyl and introduced him to Ardmore & Beechwood, a music publisher based in the HMV offices. They liked what they heard and were keen to sign the publishing rights for 'Like Dreamers Do'. So, when Epstein turned up in Martin's office, he anticipated a similar positive response. Their meeting was pleasant but Epstein left with no promises.

Martin's indifference was overruled by his boss, the head of EMI Len Wood, and he was instructed to offer The Beatles a contract and bring the band in for a recording session on 6 June 1962. They brought two new songs to the session, 'Love Me Do' and 'P.S. I Love You', but despite already having secured a contract, performed nervously and tentatively. Martin, still unsure of his new signing, asked the group up to the control room to talk them through the production. Afterwards, he asked them if there was anything they didn't like. George, in this moment of tension, quipped, 'Well, for a start, I don't like your tie.' The control room collapsed into laughter, and Martin then succumbed to the full Beatle joshing experience, finally grasping exactly why the world would fall in love with them. Still, he did have reservations about their drummer, Pete Best.

In 1965, Martin left EMI to become a freelance producer. He started his own company, Associated Independent Recording

(AIR) – though he was employed to continue working with The Beatles – and made more money than he did as an EMI employee. After The Beatles split up, he continued to work with a variety of musicians, including Jeff Beck, Elton John, Kenny Rogers, Pete Townshend and Celine Dion, and opened a studio in Montserrat, though it was later destroyed in a hurricane. He reunited with Paul to work on the glorious James Bond theme 'Live And Let Die', and produced three of Paul's solo albums, *Tug Of War*, *Pipes Of Peace* and *Give My Regards To Broad Street*. As his hearing began to fail, he brought in his son, Giles, to help him with later Beatles projects, including the Las Vegas stage performance *Love* with Cirque du Soleil. George Martin died in his sleep, aged ninety, in 2016, leaving behind an extraordinary musical legacy.

15

RINGO JOINS THE BEATLES

My soul is that of a drummer . . . I didn't do it to become
rich and famous. I did it because it was the love of my life.
– Ringo Starr

After the Eddie Clayton Skiffle Group disbanded, Richy Starkey played for a while with the Darktown Skiffle Group, at that time Liverpool's biggest group. He then teamed up with Alan Caldwell, a tall, blond, athletic frontman whose unfortunate stutter disappeared as soon as he stepped on stage, and John Byrnes, a talented, maverick guitarist to play drums for their group, the Raving Texans. Al and John changed their names to Al Storm and Johnny Guitar and renamed the group Al Storm and the Hurricanes, then Jett Storm and the Hurricanes before settling on Rory Storm and the Hurricanes. Rory and his band were flash; in matching coloured suits, with Rory throwing himself about on stage, and sometimes into the crowd, they were exciting to watch. They quickly became the top band in Liverpool, sharing a residency with The Beatles in Hamburg, and were regularly booked as entertainment for Butlin's holiday camp in Pwllheli, Wales. It was here Richy Starkey became Ringo Starr and was given his own spot in the Hurricanes' set – 'Starr Time' – when he sang 'Alley Oop' or Carl Perkins' 'Matchbox'.

By the end of 1961, Ringo was fed up. Rory Storm and the Hurricanes were still popular, but their repertoire and stage show hadn't developed, and they were now eclipsed by The Beatles. He applied for an American visa, but was daunted by the number and nature of the questions on the form. When he was asked to be the house drummer in the Star Club in Hamburg backing Tony Sheridan, he ditched the emigration plans. Just before he left for Hamburg in early 1962, he was brought in to play with The Beatles for their Cavern Christmas show as Pete Best had called in sick. He had always got on well with the band since sharing the stage in Hamburg, and he was happy to step in. It was a great gig, and George started pushing the idea to John, Paul and new manager Brian that Ringo join the band permanently.

His time in Hamburg was cut short by flooding, which closed the clubs in the city, and he headed back to Liverpool. He played two more gigs with The Beatles (again due to Pete's absence) and rejoined Rory Storm and the Hurricanes, who had been booked to play US Army bases in France.

Then, on 14 August 1962, just as The Hurricanes started another Butlin's stint, Ringo received a phone call. Epstein asked him to join the band – if he agreed to shave off his beard and flatten his quiff. He did, of course. Much later, Epstein described how Ringo was 'the catalyst for the others', that he 'completed the jigsaw'.

Pete Best was called in to Brian's office two days later and told the news. He was offered a place in another band, which he declined.

Later that week, Ringo joined The Beatles for their gig at Hulme Hall in the Wirral where, according to onlookers, they never sounded better. On Sunday, they were due to play back on their home turf, at the Cavern. There were many grumpy Pete Best fans shouting, 'Pete Best forever, Ringo never,' and Epstein's car was vandalised, but, in time, Ringo won them over.

16

THE FIFTH BEATLE

NEIL ASPINALL

*My first encounter with George was behind the school
air-raid shelters. This great mass of shaggy hair loomed up
and an out-of-breath voice requested a quick drag of my
Woodbine. It was one of the first cigarettes either of us had
smoked. We spluttered our way through it bravely but gleefully.*
— Neil Aspinall

Neil Stanley Aspinall was born on 13 October 1941 in Prestatyn,
Wales, where his mother had been evacuated during the air raids
in Liverpool. His father missed the birth as he was serving with
the Navy.

Mother and baby arrived back in Liverpool in 1942. After
passing the eleven-plus, he gained a place at the Liverpool Institute
where he was in the same class as Paul for English and art. He met
George at school, but by the end of his schooling, it was Pete Best
who was his closest friend.

He left the institute with eight GCEs and started to train as an
accountant, but as Pete and The Beatles got more and more gigs,
he left his traineeship to become the band's full-time driver and
assistant. He also moved in as a lodger to the Best family home
where he began an affair with Pete's mother, Mona.

In July 1962, Mona gave birth to Vincent 'Roag' Best, and

Passing the time on tour. George speaks with Neil Aspinall during a game of Monopoly. *Alamy*

though she named her husband Johnny as his father on the birth certificate, he was in fact Neil's son.

Soon after, Neil accompanied Pete to Epstein's office when Pete was told that he was being replaced. Despite his loyalties to the Best family, Neil decided to continue working for The Beatles not only as their road manager, but as a confidant, fixer and help in the studio.

After The Beatles split up, Neil continued to oversee the running of Apple Corps, taking care of the band's legacy and business – licensing deals, trademark issues – as well as bringing together the *Anthology* project. He also founded a film production company, Standby Films Ltd, with his wife. He retired from Apple in 2007, and died of lung cancer in New York City in 2008. More than anyone, Neil Aspinall knew The Beatles' secrets, but he chose to remain silent and loyal throughout his life.

17

SONGBOOK

LOVE ME DO/P.S. I LOVE YOU

A-side:
Love Me Do (Lennon-McCartney)

B-side:
P.S. I Love You (Lennon-McCartney)

Released: 5 October 1962 (Parlophone)
Highest chart position: 17
Weeks in chart: 18

FAB FACT

The single was recorded over two sessions; the first was on 4 September 1962, with only John, Paul, George and Ringo, where they recorded 'Love Me Do' and 'How Do You Do It', the latter written by Mitch Murray. At this point, George Martin was still unconvinced of the band's own songs. The Beatles were adamant, though, that they shouldn't release 'How Do You Do It', and instead recorded the B-side of 'Love Me Do', 'P.S. I Love You', in a second session on 11 September.

FAB FACT

At the session on 11 September, to Ringo's horror, George Martin brought in a session drummer, Andy White. They recorded 'Love Me Do' again, with Ringo relegated to playing the tambourine, and 'P.S. I Love You' (Ringo on maracas this time). In the end, the version of 'Love Me Do' released as their first single was the version where Ringo played the drums. The Andy White version of 'Love Me Do' appeared on The Beatles' first album, *Please Please Me*.

FAB FACT

The first publishing contract signed by John and Paul was with publishing company Ardmore & Beechwood for these two songs only, and, as Paul had been the primary writer on both, the contract was written so that the credit should be labelled McCartney-Lennon. When a new publishing contract was signed with Dick James for the release of their next single, 'Please Please Me', with the songwriters listed as Lennon-McCartney, the record was still credited as McCartney-Lennon, as were each of their self-penned songs on the *Please Please Me* album. It was only when The Beatles released 'She Loves You' that the familiar Lennon-McCartney credit stuck.

18

SONGBOOK

PLEASE PLEASE ME/ASK ME WHY

A-side:
Please Please Me (Lennon-McCartney)

B-side:
Ask Me Why (Lennon-McCartney)

Released: 11 January 1963 (Parlophone)
Highest chart position: 1
Weeks in chart: 18

FAB FACT

'Please Please Me' was influenced by Bing Crosby's 'Please', the emotional ballads of Roy Orbison, and the harmonies of The Everly Brothers. When it was first performed to George Martin it was sung at a slower tempo. He suggested they speed things up and add the harmonica that had worked so well in 'Love Me Do'.

FAB FACT

After the success of 'Love Me Do' the nerves had gone. At the recording session on 26 November 1962, The Beatles rearranged the song with Martin's suggestions, and once it was in the can, he remarked, 'Congratulations, boys, you've just recorded your first number one.'

FAB FACT

Again at Martin's suggestion, Epstein met up with music publisher Dick James. On hearing 'Please Please Me', James immediately got on the phone to the producer of the ITV show *Thank Your Lucky Stars*, and played the song to him over the phone. The band were booked, and appeared on 19 January, soon after the single's release. After the success of 'Please Please Me' James and Brian Epstein agreed to establish Northern Songs, the company that would oversee The Beatles' music publishing.

19

SONGBOOK

PLEASE PLEASE ME

*One of the greatest first albums in rock . . . an assault
of thrumming energy and impeccable vocal harmonies*
– *Rolling Stone*, 100 Best Debut Albums of All Time

*Cliff has competition . . . All told, it adds up to a respectable
debut long-player, though whether we'll still remember
them come Christmas is anyone's guess.*
– Sidney Shirley, *Record Collector*

TRACK LIST

Side 1:
I Saw Her Standing There (Lennon-McCartney)
Misery (Lennon-McCartney)
Anna (*Go To Him*) (Alexander)
Chains (Goffin-King)
Boys (Dixon-Farrell)
Ask Me Why (Lennon-McCartney)
Please Please Me (Lennon-McCartney)

Side 2:
Love Me Do (Lennon-McCartney)
P.S. I Love You (Lennon-McCartney)

Baby, It's You (David-Williams-Bacharach)
Do You Want To Know A Secret (Lennon-McCartney)
A Taste Of Honey (Scott-Marlow)
There's A Place (Lennon-McCartney)
Twist And Shout (Medley-Russell)

Released: 22 March 1963 (Parlophone)
Highest chart position: 1
Weeks in chart: 70 (30 at number 1)

FAB FACT

Early 1963 saw The Beatles on the road on a tour supporting current UK chart favourite Helen Shapiro, or playing theatre gigs set up by Epstein. But there was one day free in their touring schedule on 11 February, earmarked for recording their debut album. So, in the Abbey Road studio from ten in the morning until after ten at night, the group recorded ten more songs, on top of their two singles to make up *Please Please Me*.

FAB FACT

In the beginning Martin was keen to capture The Beatles' live sound, and he and Epstein investigated the possibility of bringing the Cavern audience to Abbey Road. In the end, this idea was shelved, though the desire to capture that energy explains Paul's excited count-in on the opening track, 'I Saw Her Standing There'.

FAB FACT

The second track on the album, 'Misery', was written by John and Paul while on the Helen Shapiro tour with the notion that they would give her the song to record. She declined, but it was recorded by Kenny Lynch – the first non-Beatle to release a Lennon-McCartney number.

'Misery' wasn't the only song from this album that would be covered by someone else. 'Do You Want To Know A Secret' was given to Billy J. Kramer (with The Dakotas), another Liverpool band managed by Epstein, and reached the top of the singles chart in June 1963.

With time ticking on their studio slot, Martin was keen to record a rabble-rousing finale. Over a last cup of tea, The Beatles decided the best song to close the album would be their cover version of The Isley Brothers' 'Twist And Shout'. Although John was suffering from a cold and had been singing all day, he nailed the song in one full-throttle take.

Please Please Me went straight to number one on its release, and was only toppled from the top spot later that same year by the second album, *With The Beatles*.

20

SONGBOOK

FROM ME TO YOU/THANK YOU GIRL

A-side:
From Me To You (Lennon-McCartney)

B-side:
Thank You Girl (Lennon-McCartney)

Released: 11 April 1963 (Parlophone)
Highest chart position: 1
Weeks in chart: 21

FAB FACT

Instructed by Martin to get writing more songs as quickly as possible, 'From Me To You' was written on the tour bus between shows on the Shapiro tour. Cleverly, they incorporated the harmonica and falsetto leap that had worked so well in 'Please Please Me'.

FAB FACT

Both songs were inspired by letter writing with 'From Me To You' taking its name from the letters page in the *NME* magazine, titled 'From You To Us', and 'Thank You Girl' influenced by their fan mail.

'From Me To You' spent seven weeks at number one, knocked off the top spot by another Epstein-managed Liverpool band, Gerry and the Pacemakers, with 'I Like It'.

21

THE FIFTH BEATLE

MAL EVANS

Bought Ringo some undies for his visit to the doctor.
– Mal Evans, diary entry, 1967

Arguably one of the most deserving of the title 'Fifth Beatle', Malcolm 'Mal' Frederick Evans was born in Liverpool on 27 May 1935. A massive Elvis Presley fan, he chanced upon The Beatles during one of their Cavern lunchtime slots while taking a break from his job as a GPO telephone engineer.

A gentle giant in thick glasses, who stood over six foot tall, he was asked to become the Cavern's doorman. He was happy to supplement his Post Office wages, as in 1961 he had a young son, Gary, and a wife, Lily, to support. He also shared driving duties with Neil Aspinall if needed.

By August 1963, with Beatlemania bubbling up, Evans was brought in full-time as a road manager and bodyguard, while Aspinall took on more of a personal assistant role with the band. The two men's characters contrasted and complemented each other: Mal was laid-back, easy-going and unfazed by The Beatles' demands; Neil was more anxious, driven and detail-oriented. Both were utterly loyal and exactly who The Beatles needed for support.

When The Beatles split up, Evans found it difficult to adjust to a new role in life. He tried producing, and moved to Los Angeles where he partied hard, particularly when his old Beatles pals were in town. In 1976, drugged out and confused, and threatening suicide with an air rifle, he was shot dead by the police at a friend's house. He had been working on his memoirs, *Living with The Beatles Legend*, at the time of his death, though they have never been published.

The ever-dependable Mal Evans dismantles Ringo' drum kit after a show. *Alamy*

22

ALL THESE PLACES HAD THEIR MOMENTS

TOURING THE UK

Destined to be regular chart entries.
– Record Retailer, 10 January 1963

It takes a lot of work to create a mania. The year 1963 saw The Beatles working 300 days out of 365, on stage performances, radio and television appearances, and in the recording studio – sometimes all three in one day. On one of those manic early days, while travelling from London to Liverpool, a stone chipped the windscreen of The Beatles' van. Instead of stopping off to get it fixed, Evans duly bashed in the entire windscreen while still driving to get the band to their destination on time. It was winter, it was freezing, so to keep warm in the back of the van, John, Paul, George and Ringo lay on top of each other in a Fab sandwich, routinely swapping positions so the Beatle on top wouldn't freeze to death.

They travelled the UK first in February as a supporting act in a package tour headlined by Helen Shapiro, and were received well after the success of 'Love Me Do' and 'Please Please Me'. They followed this in March and April with another package tour supporting US stars Chris Montez and Tommy Roe, and were swiftly moved up the bill when it became clear where the audience's allegiance lay – they had just sent 'From Me To You' to number one after all. Their last package tour took place in the summer when they were given equal billing with Roy Orbison. They closed the show on each date, and got their first million-selling single in 'She Loves You'.

In between package tours, and afterwards, they played their own shows and also took part in their first international tour, travelling around Sweden in October. When they landed back at London Airport, they were greeted by 10,000 (some accounts say 20,000) screaming fans, and held up the travel plans of Prime Minister Sir Alec Douglas-Home and Miss World. By the autumn, the crowd reactions were making the news: in Plymouth, the crowd were hosed down in an effort to control them, and, in Birmingham, The Beatles had to escape the theatre disguised as policemen.

Their success had a knock-on effect on the careers of other Liverpool bands managed by Epstein and recorded by Martin. Both Gerry and the Pacemakers and Billy J. Kramer and the Dakotas topped the UK chart – in fact, in thirty-seven weeks in 1963, George Martin productions hit the number one spot.

By Christmas, The Beatles had their fourth number one, 'I Want To Hold Your Hand', a second number one album, *With The Beatles*, had stormed the Palladium and the Royal Command Performance, and were playing a sold-out Christmas run in London with their Liverpool buddies Cilla Black, Billy J. Kramer, Tommy Quickly and The Fourmost. They were also immortalised in the song 'All I Want For Christmas Is A Beatle' by future sitcom star Dora Bryan. Beatlemania had arrived.

23

SONGBOOK

SHE LOVES YOU/I'LL GET YOU

A-side:
She Loves You (Lennon-McCartney)

B-side:
I'll Get You (Lennon-McCartney)

Released: 23 August 1963 (Parlophone)
Highest chart position: 1
Weeks in chart: 33

FAB FACT

'She Loves You' remains the bestselling single by The Beatles, the bestselling single of 1963 and the bestselling single of the sixties in the UK.

FAB FACT

'She Loves You' was written and recorded in a week, while the band were on tour with Roy Orbison and Gerry and the Pacemakers. Serenading the tour bus, when John and George shook their heads while singing the falsetto 'oooh', the other musicians burst out laughing. Many were sceptical about the 'yeah, yeah, yeah' refrain too – Paul's dad suggested they should stay away from

Americanisms – but John was certain it would work on stage so they kept it in. He was right.

FAB FACT
'She Loves You' had two stints at the top of the charts, for four weeks after release and for another two weeks in late November. It was knocked off the top spot the second time around by their next single, 'I Want To Hold Your Hand'.

24

ALL THESE PLACES HAD THEIR MOMENTS

SUNDAY NIGHT AT THE LONDON PALLADIUM
AND THE ROYAL COMMAND PERFORMANCE

*I cracked a joke on stage. I was fantastically nervous, but I wanted
to say something to rebel a bit, and that was the best I could do.*
– John Lennon

Two events in 1963 cemented Beatlemania as a phenomenon. All
year, the band had been travelling around the country gaining
more fans everywhere they went; those fans were then trotting
off to buy Beatles records in impressive numbers. The music press
were sympathetic, but the mainstream newspapers were well
behind the kids in recognising the scale of what was happening.

Then, on 13 October, The Beatles were invited to top the bill on
the BBC's *Sunday Night at the London Palladium*, a pinnacle in the
world of British light entertainment. Such was the show's reputation,
that appearing on the bill was a running joke in the Starkey
household; family friend Annie Maguire started it after Ringo first
started to play the drums. Ringo was so mindful of this memory
that he was sick with nerves on the night of their performance.

Before The Beatles took to the stage to perform 'From Me
To You', 'I'll Get You', 'She Loves You' and 'Twist And Shout',
the fans were there in force. They'd arrived at the theatre early,
determined to get a glimpse of their new favourite group, and

the police, who had underestimated the turnout, could barely control the situation. Reporters and TV news teams were quickly despatched to see what all the fuss was about. When the show started, compere Bruce Forsyth teased them with a tantalising glimpse of John, Paul, George and Ringo before announcing, 'If you want to see them again, they'll be back in forty-two minutes.' The show was watched by 15 million viewers at home, and the press had a field day – the *Mirror* the first to coin the word 'Beatlemania' to describe the frenzy.

Next month, on 4 November, The Beatles confirmed their new standing with their iconic turn at the Royal Command Performance, attended that year by the Queen Mother, Princess Margaret and Lord Snowdon. Despite being the act everyone was talking about, The Beatles were nervous, especially as the audience was not full of the enthusiastic young kids they were used to. They sang 'From Me To You', 'She Loves You' and 'Till There Was You', hamming up their bows between each song, and then, before their last song, 'Twist And Shout', John tossed off the brilliant quip: 'Will the people in the cheaper seats clap their hands, and the rest of you, if you can just rattle your jewellery?' (This was a cleaned-up version of his original idea to tell the audience to 'rattle their fucking jewellery', much to Epstein's horror.) Asked back every year they were together, The Beatles refused.

The Royal Command Performance gained 26 million viewers and once more the tabloids couldn't get enough Beatles copy. The broadsheets joined in too, either to interpret the behaviour of the crying, screaming, fainting girls or to show appreciation of the 'aolian cadences' and 'pentatonic clusters' in The Beatles' repertoire. With the UK and much of Europe in the bag, another audience beckoned . . .

25

SONGBOOK

WITH THE BEATLES

*If there are any Beatle-haters left in Britain, I doubt they'll remain
unmoved after hearing* With The Beatles. *I'll even go this far: if
it doesn't stay at the top of the NME LP Chart for at least eight
weeks, I'll walk up and down Liverpool's Lime Street carrying an
'I Hate The Beatles' sandwich-board.*
– NME

*One gets the impression that they think simultaneously of harmony
and melody, so firmly are the major tonic sevenths and ninths built
into their tunes, and the flat submediant key switches, so natural is
the Aeolian cadence at the end of 'Not A Second Time' (the chord
progression which ends Mahler's Song of the Earth).*
– William Mann, The Times

One hopes they will be with us for a year or two yet.
– Ian McCann, Record Collector

TRACK LIST

Side 1
It Won't Be Long (Lennon-McCartney)
All I've Got To Do (Lennon-McCartney)
All My Loving (Lennon-McCartney)

Don't Bother Me (Harrison)
Little Child (Lennon-McCartney)
Till There Was You (Willson)
Please Mister Postman (Holland)

Side 2:
Roll Over Beethoven (Berry)
Hold Me Tight (Lennon-McCartney)
You Really Got A Hold On Me (Robinson)
I Wanna Be Your Man (Lennon-McCartney)
Devil In Her Heart (Drapkin)
Not A Second Time (Lennon-McCartney)
Money (*That's What I Want*) (Bradford-Gordy)

Released: 22 November 1963 (Parlophone)
Highest chart position: 1
Weeks in chart: 50 (21 at number 1)

FAB FACT

It was tough fitting in recording sessions to The Beatles' 1963 schedule, but the success of *Please Please Me* made it obvious that the band would have to record another album of original songs and cover versions from their live repertoire. The album was recorded in snatched sessions in July, September and October.

FAB FACT

The band had no say on the album artwork for *Please Please Me*, but from *With The Beatles* onwards, they were consulted on cover art. For *With The Beatles*, photographer Robert Freeman – whose striking portraits of jazz musicians had made a strong impression on Epstein – was briefed to copy the photographic style of their friends from Hamburg, Astrid Kirchherr and Jürgen Vollmer. He photographed them without a make-up artist, stylist or hairdresser in a Bournemouth hotel room when they were on tour.

(Ringo was asked to stand in the right corner of the frame and bend his knee. 'He was the last to join the group, he was the shortest and he was the drummer,' said Freeman.)

FAB FACT

With The Beatles is the first album to have a Harrison original, 'Don't Bother Me'. He was under the weather and wrote the song in the Bournemouth hotel where the cover photograph was taken.

FAB FACT

Smokey Robinson was an early influence on John and Paul's songwriting, and the songs 'Not A Second Time' and 'All I've Got To Do' were written with him in mind. The album also features a brilliant cover version – arguably one of their best – of Robinson's 'You Really Got A Hold On Me'.

FAB FACT

With The Beatles smashed the record for advance order copies, which had been held by Elvis Presley's *Blue Hawaii*.

26

SONGBOOK

I WANT TO HOLD YOUR HAND/THIS BOY

A-side:
I Want To Hold Your Hand (Lennon-McCartney)

B-side:
This Boy (Lennon-McCartney)

Released: 29 November 1963 (Parlophone)
Highest chart position: 1
Weeks in chart: 22

FAB FACT

'I Want To Hold Your Hand' was the first UK single with advance orders of one million copies. It went straight to the top of the charts, displacing 'She Loves You', spending five weeks at number one and becoming The Beatles' first Christmas number one.

FAB FACT

In late 1963, Paul was living in the family home of his new girlfriend, actress Jane Asher. Epstein had encouraged John and Paul to write a new single with the US market in mind, and in response they wrote 'I Want To Hold Your Hand' in the Ashers' music room.

FAB FACT

Capitol, the US label owned by EMI (owners of Parlophone), had, so far, passed on releasing each Beatles single in America. But by the time of 'I Want To Hold Your Hand', and the news from the UK and Europe about the band's growing popularity, they could no longer refuse. They released the single with 'I Saw Her Standing There' as its B-side on 26 December 1963. It reached the top of the charts, the fourth release by a UK artist to do so, the first three being 'Auf Wiederseh'n, Sweetheart' by Vera Lynn, 'Strangers On The Shore' by Acker Bilk, and 'Telstar' by The Tornados.

27

CRACKING AMERICA

Always America seemed too big, too vast,
too remote and too American.
– Brian Epstein

As 1964 began, the UK press had decided The Beatles were over. 'I Want To Hold Your Hand' had been ousted from the top of the charts by The Dave Clark Five's 'Glad All Over'. They were from Tottenham, Liverpool was yesterday's news, and normal entertainment service would resume, thank you very much.

The Beatles travelled to Paris on 15 January for a three-week residency at the Olympia. The first few shows were lukewarm, attended by French dignitaries rather than screaming fans, and plagued by technical difficulties. Then, one evening, while the band were winding down in their hotel room after a show, Epstein came through to tell them that 'I Want To Hold Your Hand' was number one in America. The band were ecstatic and partied into the night.

Epstein had been working hard to crack the US market, visiting New York in late 1963 on a charm offensive. While there, he met Ed Sullivan, who had seen the airport reception that greeted The Beatles when they returned from their Swedish tour, and Sullivan agreed that the band could appear on the show on 9 and 16 February. Epstein insisted that The Beatles top the bill, and although Sullivan wasn't completely convinced, he agreed.

At the same time, a young agent, Sid Bernstein, who, as a

political science student had got into the habit of reading British newspapers, got in touch with Epstein. He wanted to book The Beatles to play New York's Carnegie Hall on 12 February. He was chancing his arm – he had no agreement with the concert hall in place – but when Epstein agreed, he got to work.

'I Want To Hold Your Hand' entered the US charts at number eighty-three, moving up to forty-two the following week, then number three, and then the coveted top spot. By the time it got to number one, the single was selling 10,000 copies a day in New York alone. With The Beatles due to touch down on 7 February, Epstein insisted that Capitol spend big on promoting the trip. They obliged by plastering five million *The Beatles Are Coming* posters across the country, giving every single US radio DJ free copies of every single The Beatles had recorded to date, and sending out a million four-page newspapers on the band to as many media outlets as they could. *Life* magazine and *Newsweek* journalists were sent over to Paris to interview the band for advance features, and even Janet Leigh (of *Psycho* fame) was persuaded into wearing a Beatles wig.

Despite the massive publicity campaign, on the flight over to the US, The Beatles were anxious. Too many UK acts had gone over there and sunk without trace. They needn't have worried. On landing at JFK airport, they were greeted by 10,000 adoring fans singing 'We love you, Beatles, oh yes, we do' and a rabid, noisy press contingent itching to be unimpressed. Ushered into the airport for their introductory press conference, The Beatles could have been overawed. Instead, they bossed the room.

'There's some doubt that you can sing.'

'No, we need money first.'

'How do you account for your success?'

'A good press agent.'

'Why does your music excite them so much?'

'We don't know.'

'If we did we'd form another group and be managers.'

'How many of you are bald that you have to wear those wigs?'

'Oh, we're all bald. Don't tell anyone, please.'

'And deaf and dumb too.'

'Are you for real?'

'Come and have a feel.'

'Are you part of a social rebellion against the older generation?'

'It's a dirty lie.'

'What about the movement in Detroit to stamp out The Beatles?'

An excited crowd gathers in New York as Beatlemania strikes in the US. *Alamy*

'We have a campaign to stamp out Detroit.'

'What do you think of Beethoven?'

'Great. Especially his poems.'

The chaos followed them to the Plaza Hotel. As well as the Maysles brothers, who were documenting the trip for UK television, and more members of the media, they were welcomed by representatives of Pepsi, who presented them with branded radios so they could listen to the city's stations, all charting the band's every move. Such was the bedlam, the Plaza issued notices saying that Beatles wigs were banned from the public areas of the hotel, and they even advertised for other hotels to take The Beatles and their entourage off their hands.

The Beatles' appearances on *The Ed Sullivan Show* in New York and Miami were record-breaking, and the Carnegie Hall shows sold out in hours with Bernstein boasting he had to turn down ticket requests from David Niven and Shirley MacLaine. With screaming fans and the media in their wake, the band also travelled to Washington to play the sold-out Coliseum. British Prime Minister Alec Douglas-Home decided to postpone his visit to President Lyndon Johnson; when he did eventually arrive at the White House, he was greeted with the comment, 'I liked your advance party, but don't you think they need haircuts?'

When The Beatles returned to the UK, they left behind a totally smitten America. Fans bought up as many releases as they could, with even 'My Bonnie' finding itself in the *Billboard* Hot 100 for six weeks and reaching number twenty-six. By mid-April The Beatles had fifteen songs in the Hot 100 and occupied the top five chart positions with 'Can't Buy Me Love', 'Twist And Shout', 'She Loves You', 'I Want To Hold Your Hand' and 'Please Please Me'.

28

♪ ♪ ♪ ♪

ALL THESE PLACES HAD THEIR MOMENTS

THE ED SULLIVAN SHOW

I've heard that while the show was on there were no reported crimes, or very few. When The Beatles were on Ed Sullivan, *even the criminals had a rest for ten minutes.*
– George Harrison

The Beatles' *Ed Sullivan* appearances have now gone down in history as among the most influential moments in 20th-century broadcasting history. Even Billy Graham, the world's most famous

Ringo dances as the band rehearse for
The Ed Sullivan Show in Miami Beach. *Getty Images*

evangelist, broke his own tradition of no television on the Sabbath to watch the Fab Four. In advance of the New York show, 50,000 fans applied to get their hands on one of the 728 tickets.

On the night before the band played, Ed Sullivan read out a telegram from Elvis Presley wishing them the best of luck – a baton passed. It was less than ten years ago that Elvis had made his first appearance on the same show, famously filmed from the waist up.

A staggering 73 million people watched The Beatles on 9 February 1964. They played, live, 'All My Loving', 'Till There Was You', 'She Loves You', 'I Saw Her Standing There' and 'I Want To Hold Your Hand'.

A week later, in Miami, 75 million people watched their second live appearance, the setlist 'She Loves You', 'This Boy', 'All My Loving', 'I Saw Her Standing There', 'From Me To You' and 'I Want To Hold Your Hand'.

29

THE FIFTH BEATLE

MURRAY THE K

Sounds terrific! Take a listen!
– DJ Murray the K

Murray Kaufman, known in the US as Murray the K, was born in New York City on 14 February 1922. His mother played piano on the vaudeville circuit, and pushed him into a career as a child actor, before sending him off to military boarding school.

During the Second World War he arranged entertainment for the troops, and afterwards moved into public relations, radio production and working as a co-host at the AM radio station WMCA. He then moved to WINS in New York where he hit his stride, at first on the all-night show and then his own 7–11 p.m. slot, where he remained until early 1965. Wise-cracking, charismatic, and one of the first DJs to incorporate sound effects and jingles, he became an early fan of The Beatles, and used his gift of the gab to work his way into their inner circle. He showed them a good time in New York, taking them to the Peppermint Lounge with The Ronettes, and broadcast his shows from the band's hotel rooms in New York, Washington and Miami. It was during these broadcasts that he gave himself – thus inventing – the moniker 'The Fifth Beatle'. John was never happy about people using the title, stating, 'The Beatles are The Beatles.'

Murray the K continued to work as a radio DJ and TV producer throughout the sixties and seventies, before ill health forced him to retire in the late seventies. He died of cancer in 1982, and was inducted into the National Radio Hall of Fame in 1997.

30

WHEN THE BEATLES MET CASSIUS CLAY

Clay completely overwhelmed The Beatles, shouting, 'Who's the greatest? I'm the greatest. You're pretty, but I'm prettier.' He made them lie down, stand up, run around the ring. They had never taken a backseat before.
– Harry Benson

While in Miami, the Scottish photographer Harry Benson, who had been travelling with The Beatles on their US trip, organised a press call with the band and the contender for the world heavyweight boxing title, Cassius Clay.

The Beatles had mentioned that they'd like to meet the current champion, Sonny Liston, but he was not interested in meeting those 'bums', so Benson thought getting them together with Clay would be the next best thing. Clay was in training at the 5th Street Gym, and, as ever, intuitively aware of the publicity opportunity.

The Beatles, not exactly shrinking violets themselves, were stunned by Clay. In the ring, he ordered them around, making sure he was the main star of the photographs. He called Paul 'the pretty one' but told him, 'You're not as pretty as me.' The press lapped it up.

The photographs from the encounter are extraordinarily iconic, capturing two global phenomena together just as their cultural impact was blossoming. Despite the smiles and kidding around, The Beatles were not too pleased at being overshadowed by the ebullient boxer, particularly John; he didn't speak to Benson for a month.

The Beatles take a blow from Cassius Clay while visiting his training camp in Miami Beach. *Alamy*

31

SONGBOOK

CAN'T BUY ME LOVE/YOU CAN'T DO THAT

A-side:
Can't Buy Me Love (Lennon-McCartney)

B-side:
You Can't Do That (Lennon-McCartney)

Released: 20 March 1964 (Parlophone)
Highest chart position: 1
Weeks in chart: 15

FAB FACT

The advance orders in the UK and the US for 'Can't Buy Me Love' reached three million copies, which meant it went straight to number one on both sides of the Atlantic. It stayed there for three weeks in the UK and five weeks in the US, where it had been released four days earlier.

FAB FACT

'Can't Buy Me Love' was written in the George IV Hotel, Paris, and recorded in the EMI studios during The Beatles' residency in the city at the beginning of the year. Other recordings during these sessions were the German versions of 'She Loves You' ('Sie Liebt

Dich') and 'I Want To Hold Your Hand' ('Komm Gib Mir Deine Hand').

'Can't Buy Me Love' wasn't supposed to feature in *A Hard Day's Night* as it was released as a single before the film came out. The scene where The Beatles escape rehearsals to mess about in a nearby park was supposed to be accompanied by 'I'll Cry Instead', but director, Richard Lester, deemed the song too melancholy and replaced it with the more upbeat 'Can't Buy Me Love'.

Ella Fitzgerald's cover version of 'Can't Buy Me Love', recorded for her *Hello, Dolly!* album, was released in the UK only a month later, peaking at number 34 in the charts. Bewilderingly, it didn't crack the *Billboard* Hot 100 in the US.

32

♪†♪†♪

ON THE SILVER SCREEN

A HARD DAY'S NIGHT

The Citizen Kane *of jukebox musicals*
– *The Village Voice*, annual film poll, January 1965

In late 1963, United Artists realised that The Beatles' contract with EMI didn't include film soundtracks. They decided that they would capitalise on the success of the band – they could be a flash-in-the-pan phenomenon after all – by producing a jukebox musical on the cheap, in time for a summer release in 1964 and expressly with the aim of getting a soundtrack album on the back of it.

The Beatles were keen, but adamant that the film reflected their own sensibilities. Richard Lester was brought in to direct – he had previously worked with Peter Sellers and Spike Milligan on *The Running Jumping & Standing Still Film* – and they also suggested that up-and-coming screenwriter Alun Owen be brought in to write the script. He was of Welsh heritage but schooled in Liverpool, and had recently written the Armchair Theatre television play *No Trams to Lime Street* that the band rated. He was invited to spend a few days with The Beatles to get a sense of their characters and turns of phrase so that he could put words in their mouths that they were likely to say. While travelling with them, he noticed that they barely had time to enjoy their success and conceived a story set in 'a train and a room, a car and a room, and a room and a room'.

Costing £175,000 to make, the film took just over seven weeks to film in Twickenham Studios and various locations across London, Surrey and Newton Abbot. We follow the band over two days as they travel to London to rehearse for and play a gig, accompanied by Paul's rascal of a grandfather, played by Wilfrid Brambell, and their two assistants, Norm and Shake (fictionalised versions of Neil and Mal played by Norman Rossington and John Junkin). They dodge fans and hangers-on, try (and fail) to keep Paul's grandfather out of trouble, cheek their way through cases of mistaken identity, rescue Ringo from trouble, and generally worry both Norm and the jumpy, paranoid show producer, played by Victor Spinetti.

A Hard Day's Night premiered at the London Pavilion on 6 July 1964. Princess Margaret and Lord Snowdon were in attendance and 12,000 screaming fans crowded Piccadilly Circus. The film also had a premiere in Liverpool days later with 200,000 fans lining the streets as The Beatles made their way from the airport to a civic reception in the town hall.

United Artists were well rewarded for their prescience: *A Hard Day's Night* made $8 million in its first week of release. The film garnered two Oscar nominations for Best Screenplay and Best Score as well as positive reviews, with *The Village Voice* declaring it 'the *Citizen Kane* of jukebox musicals', which, of course, sounds hyperbolic. Nonetheless, it was unusual for a pop music film to make reference to Shakespeare and Irish republicanism, and satirise the emerging pop culture capitalism, and all underpinned by The Beatles' charm, sense of fun and infectious music.

33

SONGBOOK

A HARD DAY'S NIGHT/THINGS WE SAID TODAY

A-side:
A Hard Day's Night (Lennon-McCartney)

B-side:
Things We Said Today (Lennon-McCartney)

Released: 10 July 1964 (Parlophone)
Highest chart position: 1
Weeks in chart: 13 (3 at number 1)

FAB FACT

The title 'A Hard Day's Night' came from Ringo, who was known for his 'Ringoisms', coming up with odd but winning turns of phrase. Both the band and Richard Lester loved the phrase, with Lester deciding it was to be the film's title. The band were then asked to write a song using the title.

FAB FACT

John wrote 'A Hard Day's Night' on the very night the film title was decided, possibly so quick off the mark as a response to Paul getting the previous A-side in 'Can't Buy Me Love'. The song was recorded at Abbey Road the day after the police chase scenes were filmed in Notting Hill.

The distinctive opening chord of the song has been much debated over the decades. Was it announcing the beginning of The Beatles' imperial phase of their career? Its composition has been analysed by musicologists and mathematicians to work out the ingredients behind its powerful, unique sound.

34

SONGBOOK

A HARD DAY'S NIGHT

If you had to explain The Beatles' impact to a stranger, you'd play them the soundtrack to A Hard Day's Night. *The songs, conceived in a hotel room in a spare couple of weeks between up-ending the British class system and conquering America, were full of bite and speed. There was adventure, knowingness, love, and abundant charm.*
– Bob Stanley, *Yeah Yeah Yeah: The Story of Modern Pop*

Here it is, at last! The long-awaited title song from the Beatles' film A Hard Day's Night. *I'm sure every NME reader already has a copy on order, so you don't need me to recommend you to buy it. It's a bouncy finger-snapper, with a pounding beat and catchy melody. Both sides written by the Lennon-McCartney partnership, of course.*
– NME

TRACK LIST

Side 1
A Hard Day's Night (Lennon-McCartney)
I Should Have Known Better (Lennon-McCartney)
If I Fell (Lennon-McCartney)
I'm Happy Just To Dance With You (Lennon-McCartney)
And I Love Her (Lennon-McCartney)

Tell Me Why (Lennon-McCartney)
Can't Buy Me Love (Lennon-McCartney)

Side 2:
Any Time At All (Lennon-McCartney)
I'll Cry Instead (Lennon-McCartney)
Things We Said Today (Lennon-McCartney)
When I Get Home (Lennon-McCartney)
You Can't Do That (Lennon-McCartney)
I'll Be Back (Lennon-McCartney)

Released: 10 July 1964 (Parlophone)
Highest chart position: 1
Weeks in chart: 38 (21 at number 1)

FAB FACT

A Hard Day's Night is the only Beatles album made up entirely of
Lennon-McCartney originals.

FAB FACT

During their Paris residency in January 1964, the band bought
Bob Dylan's *Freewheelin'* album and played it constantly. *A Hard
Day's Night* is the first Beatles album composed under Dylan's
influence. You can hear the influence in the lyrics which were
introspective and uncertain – particularly in John's songs – despite
the upbeat arrangements.

FAB FACT

'You Can't Do That' was supposed to feature in the concert
sequence in the film, but was cut. It still remains a highlight on
the album.

35

JOHN LENNON, AUTHOR

*Fascinating . . . it goes down like pure whimsy
and then back-kicks like a sick mule.*
– The Sunday Times on *In His Own Write*

From boyhood, John liked to write and draw. He designed his own comic called *The Daily Howl* in which he would lampoon teachers, draw pictures and write nonsense poems and stories influenced by his love for Lewis Carroll, James Thurber and Ronald Searle.

In 1964, up-and-coming editorial director at Jonathan Cape, Tom Maschler, approached John to put together a collection of his work, which Maschler agreed to call *In His Own Write*. (Other titles that fell by the wayside included *The Transistor Negro*, *Left Hand, Left Hand* and *Stop One and Buy Me*.) The collection, with an introduction by Paul, contained thirty-one stories, poems and skits such as 'No Flies on Frank', 'Sad Michael' and 'The Wrestling Dog', all shot through with clever wordplay and grotesque imagery. It was released in March 1964 and shot to the top of the bestseller chart, outselling Ian Fleming's latest Bond novel, *You Only Live Twice*.

He was honoured with a Foyles Literary Lunch on 23 April, with demand for tickets the highest the bookshop had known. He attended with his wife, Cynthia, and Epstein, and was unaware that he was expected to make a speech. He stood up and mumbled,

'Thank you. You've got a lucky face,' before Epstein took over and said a few words to the puzzled audience.

That experience didn't put him off, and he was contracted to deliver another book, so he carried on, writing most of what became his second book, *A Spaniard in the Works*, while on holiday in Tahiti with Cynthia, George and his new girlfriend, Pattie Boyd. (George and Pattie met while filming *A Hard Day's Night*. She was playing a schoolgirl and had one line: 'Prisoners.') The stories in John's second book were longer, more ambitious and showcased his literary influences, including a Sherlock Holmes parody 'The Singularge Experience of Miss Anne Duffield'.

John Lennon arrives at the Foyles Literary Lunch
in honour of his first book *In His Own Write*. *Alamy*

36

THE FIFTH BEATLE

JIMMIE NICOL

Standing in for Ringo was the worst thing that ever happened to me.
– Jimmie Nicol

The third of June was the day before The Beatles were due to start their tour of Denmark, Holland, Hong Kong, Australia and New Zealand. At a photo shoot in London, Ringo collapsed and was rushed to hospital: the diagnosis tonsillitis and pharyngitis. Epstein was keen that the show go on – a lot of money was riding on its success – and discussed with George Martin a possible temporary replacement. George threatened to boycott the tour if it went ahead without Ringo, but he was outvoted. Martin suggested Jimmie Nicol. He'd worked with him when recording Tommy Quickly, and Nicol had also played on *Beatlemania*, a budget cover-version album released earlier that year. After a quick phone call, an afternoon's rehearsal and a Beatles haircut, Jimmie found himself in the most famous band in the world.

James George Nicol was born in London on 3 August 1939. In his childhood and teens, he drummed with the Boys' Brigade and an army cadets' military band, and, in 1957, he was spotted by impresario Larry Parnes in the 2i's coffee bar. Parnes asked Nicol to join Colin Hicks and the Cabin Boys, Colin being the younger brother of his top star, Tommy Steele. They released three singles

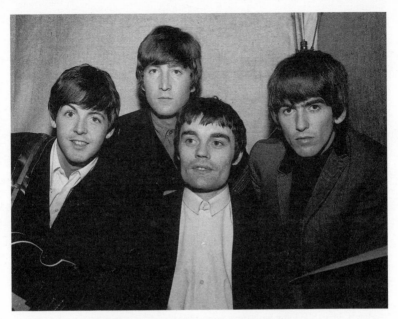
John, Paul and George with Jimmy Nicol. *Alamy*

in 1957 and 1958, though none of them bothered the charts. Nicol also played with another Parnes protégé, Vince Eager, and for Oscar Rabin's and Cyril Stapleton's bands.

By 1964, when he got the call from Martin, he had his own band, the Shubdubs, as well as playing with Georgie Fame as one of his Blue Flames, but he was happy to sign up and sample life at the centre of Beatlemania.

He travelled with them to Denmark, Holland and Hong Kong, and played with them in Adelaide, before Ringo joined the band again in Melbourne. In the twelve days that Nicol had been a Beatle, extra telephone switchboards had been installed in London to cope with fans around the world checking in on Ringo's health, and the US girl group The Bon Bons released a novelty B-side called 'What's Wrong With Ringo'.

The Beatles were fast asleep when Jimmie Nicol left to catch his plane home, but Epstein gave him a cheque for his services (reportedly £2,500 per gig, plus a £2,500 signing fee – £15,000 in total) and a watch engraved with the message 'From The Beatles and Brian Epstein to Jimmie – with appreciation and gratitude'.

Nicol was sure that his time with The Beatles would lead to bigger and better things. He subbed for Dave Clark of The Dave Clark Five when he too was hospitalised, turned down rejoining Georgie Fame and the Blue Flames, and got the Shubdubs back together. Unfortunately, the Beatle sheen had dimmed and their singles tanked, and Nicol was declared bankrupt in 1965, only nine months after his stint with The Beatles. He joined a Swedish group, The Spotnicks, for a while, though left them when his drug habit got too much for him. Taking time out of music, he dabbled in various business ventures including renovating houses, and was mistakenly declared dead in 1988. He remains out of the limelight. Rumours have him living in either London or Mexico.

37

ALL THESE PLACES HAD THEIR MOMENTS

THE FIRST WORLD TOUR

The Beatles belonged to every teenage girl. I feel like I was there at the birth of pop music. The Beatles are the Book of Genesis.
– Linda Grant, novelist and Beatlemaniac

If the first half of 1964 confirmed their new-found status, the second half of the year saw them discover just what that status *really* meant as they travelled the world, playing to their fans. Beatlemania had gone global.

In June, having left Ringo behind, on their first stop in Denmark, they had to contend with a stage invasion at the recording of a television show; in Amsterdam 100,000 people lined the canals as The Beatles waved from a barge, the police periodically fishing out those fans who had jumped in to get a closer look.

In Australia, with Ringo having rejoined the band, 300,000 fans greeted them in the streets of Adelaide and 50,000 fans applied for the 12,000 tickets available.

On their second visit to the US, in August 1964, they toured for thirty-two days, in twenty-four cities, giving thirty performances. The shows in Cleveland, Ohio and Kansas City had to be stopped to get the frenzied crowds under control. In Philadelphia, they were distressed to notice that their audience was all white. In Florida, they refused to go on unless the audience was integrated.

In Los Angeles, Martin was sent to their show in the Hollywood Bowl to record a live album. Sadly, it had to be scrapped, as the technology at the time couldn't drown out the screaming. *The Beatles At The Hollywood Bowl* was eventually released in 1977, though it was made using recordings from both their 1964 and 1965 shows at the venue.

It was almost a relief to get back to touring the ballrooms of the UK in October, dates organised by Epstein before The Beatles began filling bigger venues worldwide. They ended the year as they had begun it, with a run of Christmas shows in London and number one spots in both the singles and album charts.

38

WHEN THE BEATLES MET BOB DYLAN

*At the Delmonico, they were passing one another at a time when
each of them would have quite liked to have been the other one.*
— Mark Ellen

On Friday, 28 August 1964, The Beatles and Epstein were
relaxing in their hotel room in Delmonico's in New York. Next
door, publicist Derek Taylor was holding court with journalists,
broadcasters and musicians keen to meet the Fab Four.

Instead, Mal Evans was instructed to usher in three visitors:
writer Al Aronowitz, Victor Maymudes and Bob Dylan. The
Beatles and Dylan were fans of each other's work, and were happy
to drink, chat and joke around. When the refreshments were
offered — Dylan asked for cheap wine, but Epstein could only offer
champagne — both Aronowitz and Dylan suggested they smoke
grass instead. Famously, Dylan had misheard the lyric 'I can't hide'
in 'I Want To Hold Your Hand' as 'I get high', and thought The
Beatles old hands with marijuana. They had come across the drug
in Liverpool, but had stuck with booze and amphetamines until
Dylan passed over a clumsily rolled joint to John. John, unsure,
passed it to Ringo, who, unaware of the etiquette, smoked the
whole thing himself, thoroughly enjoying its effect.

More joints were rolled, more drink was had, and the
atmosphere turned giddy. When the phone rang, Dylan would
answer with a 'Hello, it's Beatlemania here'. Meanwhile Brian
thought he was floating up to the ceiling. Paul, convinced he now

knew the meaning of life, instructed Evans to follow him with a notebook and pen and write down whatever he said. Later, he wrote his own note to Evans, which read: 'There are seven levels.'

John and Dylan talked at length about music, with Dylan exhorting John to pay more attention to lyrics, to write from a more introspective place; although this transition had already begun in The Beatles' music, John was ready to pay attention to the advice.

39

SONGBOOK

I FEEL FINE/SHE'S A WOMAN

A-side:
I Feel Fine (Lennon-McCartney)

B-side:
She's A Woman (Lennon-McCartney)

Released: 27 November 1964 (Parlophone)
Highest chart position: 1
Weeks in chart: 13 (5 at number 1)

FAB FACT

John wrote the song around the riff that came to him while
The Beatles were recording songs for *The Beatles For Sale*. It was
inspired by the 1961 soul song 'Watch Your Step' by Bobby
Parker, another favourite from their Liverpool days.

FAB FACT

'I Feel Fine' starts with some chewy feedback, the first time such
an effect was recorded on a major recording. Creating the sound
was a happy accident, made when John leaned his semi-acoustic
Gibson guitar against the studio.

40

SONGBOOK

BEATLES FOR SALE

The kids of AD 2000 will draw from the music much the same sense of wellbeing and warmth as we do today. For the magic of The Beatles is, I suspect, timeless and ageless . . . it is adored by the world.
— Derek Taylor, album's liner notes

We're really pleased with the record and with the new LP. There was a lousy period when we didn't seem to have any material for the LP and didn't have a single. Now we're clear of things and they're due out, it's a bit of a relief.
— John Lennon

TRACK LIST

Side 1:
No Reply (Lennon-McCartney)
I'm A Loser (Lennon-McCartney)
Baby's In Black (Lennon-McCartney)
Rock 'N' Roll Music (Berry)
I'll Follow The Sun (Lennon-McCartney)
Mr. Moonlight (Johnson)
Kansas City/Hey-Hey-Hey-Hey! (Leiber-Stoller/Penniman)

Side 2:
Eight Days A Week (Lennon-McCartney)
Words Of Love (Holly)
Honey Don't (Perkins)
Every Little Thing (Lennon-McCartney)
I Don't Want To Spoil The Party (Lennon-McCartney)
What You're Doing (Lennon-McCartney)
Everybody's Trying To Be My Baby (Perkins)

Released: 4 December 1964 (Parlophone)
Highest chart position: 1
Weeks in chart: 46 (11 at number 1)

FAB FACT

The recording of *Beatles For Sale* started in August, only a month after the release of *A Hard Day's Night*. Because of the band's hectic touring schedule, the album only had eight Lennon-McCartney originals, with the rest of the album made up of cover versions.

FAB FACT

The influence of his conversation with Bob Dylan, as well as another chat with journalist Kenneth Allsop, spurred John to develop his lyrical self-revelation with songs such as 'I'm A Loser' and 'I Don't Want To Spoil The Party' hinting at his unease with fame.

FAB FACT

Both McCartney's and Lennon's raucous versions of 'Kansas City/ Hey-Hey-Hey-Hey!' and 'Rock 'n' Roll Music' were recorded in one take.

'Eight Days A Week', earmarked for a single release until John wrote 'I Feel Fine', was written in John's Weybridge house after Paul, who usually drove himself there, arrived with a chauffeur who declared himself so busy he was working 'eight days a week'. Paul liked the phrase so much, he and John immediately wrote the song around it.

FAB FACT

Robert Freeman was brought in once again to create the album cover with the brief that the photo be taken outside and to bring in the colours of a sunset. The cover was shot in Hyde Park with The Beatles looking worn out after such a busy year. In contrast, the interior shots in the gatefold sleeve show the highlights of the year: the band on stage at the Washington Coliseum (their first US appearance) and in front of a montage of photos in Twickenham film studios where they had been watching rushes of *A Hard Day's Night*.

41

SONGBOOK

TICKET TO RIDE/YES IT IS

A-side:
Ticket To Ride (Lennon-McCartney)

B-side:
Yes It Is (Lennon-McCartney)

Released: 9 April 1965 (Parlophone)
Highest chart position: 1
Weeks in chart: 12 (3 at number 1)

FAB FACT

John wrote 'Ticket To Ride' at home in Weybridge, though the distinctive drum pattern was Paul's idea. The song was a favourite of John's, who later said he considered it the first heavy rock record. It certainly signified a new direction in his songwriting with hints of the psychedelia to come in its more reflective lyrics and droning guitars.

FAB FACT

To publicise the single, The Beatles filmed a video, to be shown on *Top of the Pops*, miming to the song. This performance found its way into an episode of *Dr Who*, 'The Executioners', where the Doctor observes historical figures through a time-travel screen. The others were Abraham Lincoln and Shakespeare.

FAB FACT

The inspiration of the song has been disputed. John said that the title came about through remembering the Hamburg days and the clean bill of health the prostitutes had to carry to work in the red light district. Paul's recollection is more prosaic, that of travelling to his cousin's pub in Ryde on the Isle of Wight.

FAB FACT

'Ticket To Ride' was the first Beatles single to break the three-minute mark.

42

ON THE SILVER SCREEN

HELP!

*We showed up a bit stoned, smiled a lot
and hoped we'd get through it. We giggled a lot.*
– Paul McCartney

The closest thing to the Marx Brothers since the Marx Brothers.
– Daily Express

In late 1964, plans unfolded for the second Beatles film. Richard Lester would be back in the director's chair, and this time he'd have a bigger budget. Lester knew the film couldn't be a colour rehash of *A Hard Day's Night*, and The Beatles wouldn't be keen to repeat themselves either. He saw a screenplay of a caper written by Marc Behm – it had just been turned down by Peter Sellers – and brought in Charles Wood, also known for his surreal humour, to Beatle it up.

Epstein insisted that – for tax reasons – they had to film in the Bahamas, the band suggested that they include skiing in the film for a new experience, and the plot sees Ringo being chased by an eastern death cult and two mad scientists who are all after a special ring that he cannot get off his finger. Despite this looser, whackier focus and storyline, Lester had the right sensibilities to negotiate the paper-thin material and the unruliness of a very stoned and very giggly Fab Four, and arguably got the best out of both.

The Beatles were supported by a talented supporting cast that included Leo McKern, Eleanor Bron, Victor Spinetti, Roy Kinnear and Patrick Cargill. Even Mal Evans found himself on screen with a cameo role as a lost Channel swimmer.

As well as Nassau, and Obertauern in Austria, filming took place in Twickenham Studios, Salisbury Plain, various locations across London, and – for the Buckingham Palace scenes – in Cliveden, Lord Astor's country pile where, just a few years earlier, Christine Keeler had met John Profumo and embarked on the affair that would scandalise the UK just as Beatlemania was kicking off.

The film premiered on 29 July 1965, with Princess Margaret and Lord Snowdon once again in attendance. Critical reaction to the film was generally positive, though not as glowing as it had been for *A Hard Day's Night*, and The Beatles themselves later admitted they didn't rate the film as highly.

Yet, despite the death cult characters raising a few eyebrows in the 21st century, *Help!* has charm and great humour – surreal, whimsical and satirical – and looks fantastic. It also anticipated the music video; later, Lester was sent a parchment scroll from MTV declaring him the 'father of music video'.

The Beatles attempt to ski while Eleanor Bron watches on during the filming of *Help!*.
Alamy

43

SONGBOOK

HELP!/I'M DOWN

A-side:
Help! (Lennon-McCartney)

B-side:
I'm Down (Lennon-McCartney)

Released: 23 July 1965 (Parlophone)
Highest chart position: 1
Weeks in chart: 14 (3 at number 1)

FAB FACT

The film started life as *Beatles 2*, then *Eight Arms to Hold You* (another Ringoism). In the seventh week of filming, Lester settled on *Help!* with the added exclamation mark as a film had already been registered without the addition of the punctuation mark. Like 'A Hard Day's Night', John started writing the song right away once the title had been set.

FAB FACT

John revealed later that despite the song being written to order, it was very much an autobiographical song. By mid-1965, he had become unsure of what his status and celebrity meant. He was eating and drinking too much – he called this time his 'Fat Elvis' period – and wrote it as a cry for help.

FAB FACT

When John first presented the song in the studio, it was a mid-tempo ballad. He was persuaded to speed it up to make it sound more commercial, a decision he later regretted.

44

THE BEATLES MEET THE QUEEN

We all kind of liked the Queen. It's an age thing.
We were kids when she was crowned,
so to us she was like a glamorous film star.
– Paul McCartney

On 12 June 1965, the news broke that all four Beatles were to be awarded The Most Excellent Order of the British Empire. It baffled them, but they were happy to accept. Some previous recipients of the MBE were not pleased with this decision, particularly those from the military and the House of Lords, and sent theirs back to Buckingham Palace in protest.

Nervous and unsure, The Beatles arrived at the palace for their investiture. When Paul and Ringo walked up to the Queen, she asked them both how long the band had been together. Without missing a beat, they broke into the first line of the old music hall song 'My Old Dutch': 'We've been together now for forty years, and it don't seem a day too much.' The Queen's thoughts on their wit have not been recorded.

Later, John claimed that to calm their nerves, they'd smoked a joint in one of the palace's bathrooms, but the others quickly refuted it, saying they'd only smoked cigarettes.

In 1969, John, who had always been the most uncomfortable with accepting the honour and said that Epstein persuaded him, returned his medal with a letter saying:

Your Majesty,

I am returning this MBE in protest against Britain's involvement in the Nigeria-Biafra thing, against our support of America in Vietnam and against Cold Turkey slipping down the charts.

With love,

John Lennon of Bag

The Beatles show off their MBEs. *Alamy*

45

SONGBOOK

HELP!

There's something of the medieval minstrels in The Beatles.
One imagines them performing beneath some bird's window.
They communicate.
– Chris Welch, *Melody Maker*

Gay, infectious romp which doesn't let up in pace or sparkle
from start to finish – with the exception of one slow track.
– Derek Johnston, *NME*

TRACK LIST

Side 1:
Help! (Lennon-McCartney)
The Night Before (Lennon-McCartney)
You've Got To Hide Your Love Away (Lennon-McCartney)
I Need You (Harrison)
Another Girl (Lennon-McCartney)
You're Going To Lose That Girl (Lennon-McCartney)
Ticket To Ride (Lennon-McCartney)

Side 2:
Act Naturally (Morrison-Russell)

It's Only Love (Lennon-McCartney)
You Like Me Too Much (Harrison)
Tell Me What You See (Lennon-McCartney)
I've Just Seen A Face (Lennon-McCartney)
Yesterday (Lennon-McCartney)
Dizzy Miss Lizzy (Williams)

Released: 6 August 1965 (Parlophone)
Highest chart position: 1
Weeks in chart: 39 (9 at number 1)

FAB FACT

Photographer Robert Freeman accompanied The Beatles during the filming of *Help!* as a consultant on colour and came up with the idea for the album cover when he watched the band larking about in the Alps. Setting up the photo shoot to recreate the white of the snow, he originally had the band spell out H-E-L-P in semaphore, but when that didn't look so good, they improvised their arm placement.

FAB FACT

Despite not appearing in the film, the song that garnered the most attention on the album's release was Paul's 'Yesterday'. He famously woke up from a dream with the melody fully formed in his head. Not believing in such good luck, he took the song round many musician friends, including Alma Cogan – known to have an encyclopaedic knowledge of standards – to ask if the melody was from an older song. Given the all-clear to the song he had named 'Scrambled Eggs', he wrote the bulk of the lyrics while on holiday with Jane Asher in Albufeira, Portugal.

After Andy White's infamous stint on the drums on 'Love Me Do' and 'P.S. I Love You', the *Help!* album was the first time The Beatles used session musicians. As well as the string quartet of Tony Gilbert, Sidney Sax, Kenneth Essex and Francisco Gabarro on 'Yesterday', Johnnie Scott was drafted in to play tenor and alto flutes on 'You've Got To Hide Your Love Away'.

During the recording sessions, The Beatles recorded two of their most famous abandoned songs, 'That Means A Lot' (later given to P. J. Proby) and 'If You've Got Troubles' (given to Ringo to sing, who was so uninspired by it that be pleads before the solo, 'Oh, rock on, anybody!').

46

👤👤👤👤

ALL THESE PLACES HAD THEIR MOMENTS

SHEA STADIUM

Once you know you've filled a place that
size, it's magic; just walls of people.
– Paul McCartney

The Beatles touched down in New York in mid-August to begin their North American tour. First stop, another appearance on *The Ed Sullivan Show*, and then, the next day, into the record books.

Shea Stadium was home to the New York Jets baseball team, but on the evening of Sunday, 15 August, 55,600 screaming Beatlemaniacs filled the stands for the first ever rock 'n' roll stadium concert. The scale of the show was brand new, as was the seriously healthy ticket sales revenue, yet The Beatles took this next milestone in their stride, the thrill of Beatlemania not quite as thrilling as it used to be.

They were supported by soul singer Brenda Holloway with the King Curtis band, Cannibal & the Headhunters, Sounds Incorporated and The Young Rascals, and introduced by Ed Sullivan. As they ran on stage in their high-collared beige jackets complete with sheriff badges, deafening screams rang out from the crowd. The audience included two future Beatle wives: Linda Eastman and Barbara Bach.

Filmed for television, the concert is a revelation of the utter chaos of Beatlemania. Witness the policeman putting his fingers in his ears as The Beatles first run out from the stadium tunnel, the hysterical girls hanging on for dear life to the stand fences, fans being slapped out of fainting fits by their friends and the policemen chasing down people on the field who had broken free from the stands. *The Beatles at Shea Stadium* was shown on BBC1, in black and white, on 1 March 1966, and in the US, in colour, on the ABC network in January 1967.

47

WHEN THE FAB FOUR MET THE KING

*If you guys are just gonna sit there
and stare at me, I'm goin' to bed.*
– Elvis Presley

As well as the highlight of the Shea Stadium concert, the 1965 tour saw The Beatles meet their all-time hero. Taking a break from their tour once they had reached Los Angeles, word came from Colonel Tom Parker that Elvis was also taking a break from shooting his latest film. So off they drove in a Cadillac limousine, along with Neil Aspinall and Elvis superfan Mal Evans, up the twisting roads to Elvis's French Regency-style mansion in Beverly Hills.

On entering the house, they were confronted by Elvis himself in front of a massive colour television – complete with remote control, much to the band's amazement – with the sound turned down. He was strumming a bass guitar, surrounded by his 'mafia', who were playing pool.

Paul described it as 'one of the great meetings of my life', and although there was no great bonding as with their first encounter with Bob Dylan, they all came away from the meeting with fond memories: of Charlie Rich's 'Mohair Sam' on repeat on the jukebox, of being introduced to Priscilla (differing recollections have her in gingham with a bow in her hair, a tiara and a full-length gown), and of poor Mal being unable to give his idol a plectrum as the pockets on his suit – where he usually kept a collection handy – had been sewn up by the dry cleaners just before the visit.

48

THE BEATLES TRIP

*It was fantastic. I felt in love, not with anything
or anybody in particular, but with everything.*
– George Harrison

In early 1965 – the exact date is unknown – John and George were invited, along with their partners Cynthia and Pattie for dinner with their dentist, John Riley. After coffee, the foursome announced they were leaving to go to a gig at the Pickwick Club, but the dentist advised them to stay put. He had laced the sugar in their coffee with lysergic acid diethylamide, the latest wheeze in Swinging London and then still legal. Confused and suspicious that he was persuading them to stay for an orgy, John, George, Cynthia and Pattie left the house and made their way to the Ad Lib club. Squeezed into George's Mini, the hallucinations kicked in. Everything around them began to expand and contract, the street lights and advertising in shops, clubs and theatres made them feel as if everything was in flames, and Pattie had an overwhelming desire to smash shop windows. The Ad Lib, then the grooviest nightspot in town, was too overwhelming despite Ringo's friendly face there. Miraculously, George managed to drive everyone back to his and Pattie's house. Cynthia was deeply upset by the experience, while George described a real connection to the world around him, and how the trip gave him and John a special bond. John drew lots of pictures, one of which he gave to Ringo – four heads all saying, 'We all agree with you.'

Egged on by John and George, Ringo was next to try the drug. He was with Neil Aspinall, during the 1965 tour, at a party in Benedict Canyon, Los Angeles. Dave Crosby and Roger McGuinn from The Byrds were present, as was Peter Fonda, who spent the evening tediously telling everyone he had shot himself and died, inspiring John to write 'She Said She Said', which appeared on *Revolver*.

Paul was the last Beatle to try acid, and took his first trip with Tara Browne, away from the peer pressure of his bandmates, in 1966. He was, however, the first to go public about the experience. In 1967, when asked by a journalist about it, he confessed, causing a flurry of criticism. Paul's second trip was with John at his house in Cavendish Avenue after the infamous recording session for *Sgt. Pepper*'s 'Getting Better'. There, John accidentally took a tab, thinking it was amphetamine – the only time LSD was taken in the studio. Panicking at the mic, John was taken to the roof by an innocent Martin, unaware of why John was feeling so fragile. George and Paul, knowing better, got him off the roof and to Paul's house nearby, where Paul kept him company on his trip.

John subsequently went in deep with LSD, taking so many trips he later said he completely destroyed his ego and had to have Derek Taylor remind him of all the things he had achieved. There is no doubt, though, that their introduction to the drug had a notable effect on their songwriting as they became increasingly interested in expanding the possibilities within the Abbey Road studio.

49

ALL THESE PLACES HAD THEIR MOMENTS

THE SECOND WORLD TOUR

*That is the main problem with fame – that people forget
how to act normally. They are not in awe of you, but in
awe of the thing you have become. It's a concept that
they have of stardom and notoriety. So they act crazy.*
– George Harrison

*I remember playing a big bullring in Barcelona, the Plaza
de Toros, where the Lord Mayor had great seats and
all the rich people had seats but the kids, our real
audience, were outside. We used to get upset about that.*
– Paul McCartney

If The Beatles' US tour in 1965 provided the seminal moments
of their record-breaking Shea Stadium appearance and encounter
with Elvis, the band were tiring of Beatlemania. They stopped
committing themselves to so many TV and radio appearances,
realising that they no longer needed to strive for the attention
they had worked so hard to achieve.

Their gigs had now taken on a feeling of a military operation
rather than a joyous celebration, with hundreds of policemen,
guards and firemen deployed to each gig, and during their
European tour they witnessed horrifying police brutality towards

their Spanish fans. Other than their record-breaking gig at Shea Stadium, many of their international gigs saw empty seats in the audience, due to heatwaves or the tickets being too expensive for the fans. Their short UK tour in December was sold out, but as music arenas and stadiums were not yet commonplace, they were still playing smaller venues, ones they had been playing for years. The Beatles were getting tired of the repetition, and after these dates they never played live in the UK again.

No longer did they need to record their music in snatched days between tours and media appearances; now they gave themselves the luxury of a month and a half of studio time to record their upcoming singles and album. And to counter all the demands for TV appearances around the world, they filmed a number of promotional films for 'I Feel Fine', 'Ticket To Ride', 'Help!', 'Day Tripper' and 'We Can Work It Out', selling them to TV stations and pioneering the music video.

The Beatles persevere through another pre-concert
press conference as they tour America. *Getty Images*

50

†††††

SONGBOOK

DAY TRIPPER/WE CAN WORK IT OUT

A-side:
Day Tripper (Lennon-McCartney)

A-side:
We Can Work It Out (Lennon-McCartney)

Released: 3 December 1965 (Parlophone)
Highest chart position: 1
Weeks in chart: 12 (5 at number 1)

FAB FACT

As recording for their new album got underway, John and Paul were 'forced' to write a single quicksmart. Musically inspired by Otis Redding, who later recorded his own version in 1967, 'Day Tripper' was mostly written by John. His lyrics satirised the London swingers who dabbled in a bohemian lifestyle but didn't commit to its radical outlook.

FAB FACT

'Day Tripper' was scheduled to be the next Beatles single until, a few days later, Paul brought in the words and music to 'We

Can Work It Out'. John added the 16-bar middle, though it was George Martin's idea to change its tempo from the rest of the song.

'We Can Work It Out' was then earmarked as the A-side, much to John's chagrin. He continued to argue that 'Day Tripper' should be the next single, so it was decided that both songs would be promoted as a double A-side. It went on to become The Beatles' fastest-selling single in the UK since 'Can't Buy Me Love'. Over in the US, 'We Can Work It Out' reached the top of the *Billboard* Hot 100, while 'Day Tripper' peaked at number five.

51

SONGBOOK

RUBBER SOUL

It was the most out-there music they'd ever made, but also their warmest, friendliest and most emotionally direct. As soon as it dropped in December 1965, Rubber Soul *cut the story of pop music in half – we're all living in the future this album invented.*
– Rob Sheffield, *Rolling Stone*, 2015

I didn't understand a word, I didn't think it was any good, and then six weeks later you couldn't live without the record. And that's good – that's when you trust the people who make music to take you somewhere you haven't been before.
– Elvis Costello

TRACK LIST

Side 1:

Drive My Car (Lennon-McCartney)

Norwegian Wood (*This Bird Has Flown*) (Lennon-McCartney)

You Won't See Me (Lennon-McCartney)

Nowhere Man (Lennon-McCartney)

Think For Yourself (Harrison)

The Word (Lennon-McCartney)

Michelle (Lennon-McCartney)

Side 2:
What Goes On (Lennon-McCartney-Starkey)
Girl (Lennon-McCartney)
I'm Looking Through You (Lennon-McCartney)
In My Life (Lennon-McCartney)
Wait (Lennon-McCartney)
If I Needed Someone (Harrison)
Run For Your Life (Lennon-McCartney)

Released: 3 December 1965 (Parlophone)
Highest chart position: 1
Weeks in chart: 42 (8 at number 1)

FAB FACT

Once again, Robert Freeman was charged with producing the album cover shot; he photographed the band in John's garden in Weybridge. When they all got together to look at the selection of shots taken, Freeman projected the images on an album-sized card to see how they would look, but the card slipped, elongating the image. They loved the distorted version even more, and it matched the album title.

FAB FACT

The title *Rubber Soul* was agreed upon as an in-joke and in solidarity – or was it a sly dig? – after the band had read a critique of the Rolling Stones as 'plastic soul'.

FAB FACT

In an interview just as recording began, Paul revealed that his and John's current songwriting development was branching out into 'comedy songs'. It is true that the songs in *Rubber Soul* take on a more narrative approach in their lyrics – songs like 'Girl' and 'Michelle' parody Greek traditional music and French chanson – and throughout the album there are cheeky flourishes in the 'beep, beep, yeah' in 'Drive My Car' and the 'tit, tit, tit' backing vocals in 'Girl'. Still, the album also reveals both Lennon and McCartney in a more contemplative mood.

FAB FACT

A highlight of the album, 'In My Life', was written mostly by John. He started to compose it as a nostalgic look back on the bus trip he made from Menlove Avenue to the centre of Liverpool, and wanted to name various people and places that meant a lot to him when he was younger. Struggling with the lyrics, once he made the decision to be less specific, the song flowed easily. In the studio, Paul helped out with the melody, and Martin contributed his distinctive solo by playing the piano at half-tempo and then speeding it up at the studio controls.

FAB FACT

The French phrases in 'Michelle' were translated for Paul by his childhood friend Ivan Vaughan's wife, Jan.

FAB FACT

Ringo was given a songwriting credit on 'What Goes On', a song John had started writing back in Liverpool. In his self-deprecating way, when Ringo was asked about his contribution he replied that he'd only written 'about five words'.

FAB FACT

'Norwegian Wood (That Bird Has Flown)' features the first appearance of an Indian sitar on a pop record after George became interested in the instrument after filming the Indian restaurant scene in *Help!* There has been much speculation about the identity of the woman: some suggest the song is about John's friendship with *London Standard* journalist Maureen Cleave, who interviewed the band many times; others identify Sonny Freeman, the German model and wife of photographer Robert Freeman. Sonny shared a flat with John and wife Cynthia, and used to describe herself as Norwegian.

52

SONGBOOK

PAPERBACK WRITER/RAIN

A-side:
Paperback Writer (Lennon-McCartney)

B-side:
Rain (Lennon-McCartney)

Released: 10 June 1966 (Parlophone)
Highest chart position: 1
Weeks in chart: 11 (2 at number 1)

FAB FACT

The year 1966 started off quietly for The Beatles; they now felt they could control their own itinerary for recording, releasing and promoting their material. 'Paperback Writer' was released a whole six months after their previous single, and although it reached the top of the charts, it was their first single since 'She Loves You' not to go straight to number one.

FAB FACT

Paul wrote the song with John at Weybridge, after reading a *Daily Mail* article about an aspiring author. He was keen to write a song based around a single chord, and swapped his usual Hofner bass for a Rickenbacker, with its heavier sound. When John and George sing the backing vocals, they are singing 'Frère Jacques'.

FAB FACT

'Rain' – considered by many to be the best Beatles B-side – was played faster and slowed down in production to give the song its dreamy, psychedelic quality.

FAB FACT

Promotional videos (in colour!) for both 'Paperback Writer' and 'Rain' were directed by Michael Lindsay-Hogg, in the 18th-century gardens of Chiswick House. In the video, you can see that Paul has chipped his front tooth (he'd had an accident on a moped).

FAB FACT

The Beatles filmed their one and only appearance on BBC's *Top of the Pops* to promote the single.

53

SONGBOOK

ELEANOR RIGBY/YELLOW SUBMARINE

A-side:
Eleanor Rigby (Lennon-McCartney)

A-side:
Yellow Submarine (Lennon-McCartney)

Released: 5 August 1966 (Parlophone)
Highest chart position: 1
Weeks in chart: 13 (4 at number 1)

FAB FACT

Where did 'Eleanor Rigby' come from? When Paul was first working on the melody, he used the name 'Miss Daisy Hawkins' for the spinster who is central to the story. 'Eleanor' came from the actress Eleanor Bron, who had worked with The Beatles on *Help!* When visiting Jane Asher, working in Bristol at the repertory theatre, Paul walked past a wine shop called Rigby & Evans Ltd, and the name was complete. Coincidentally, there is a gravestone commemorating an Eleanor Rigby in the churchyard of St Peter's Church in Woolton, Liverpool, where John and Paul met for the first time.

Further lyrics for the song came in John's house during an evening gathering with the rest of the band and Pete Shotton, John's childhood friend. George is thought to have contributed to the 'lonely people' refrain, while Ringo is credited with having Father McKenzie darning his socks in the night. Father McKenzie was originally Father McCartney, but it was changed after a skim through the phone book.

The first recording session for 'Yellow Submarine' was overseen by engineer Geoff Emerick instead of George Martin, who was ill with food poisoning. The second session, dedicated to the backing vocals and sound effects, was recorded as a party, with the band, their guests – including Pattie Harrison and Marianne Faithfull – and Abbey Road staff raiding the cupboards to help create the songs soundscape. John blew bubbles in a bucket, chauffeur Alf Bicknell shook chains in a bath, Brian Jones from the Rolling Stones clinked glasses, and everyone joined in the sing-along chorus. After the session ended, Mal Evans, with a bass drum strapped to his chest, led everyone in a conga round the studio.

54

SONGBOOK

REVOLVER

We'll lose some fans with [the new album], but we'll also gain some. The fans we'll probably lose will be the ones who like the things about us that we never liked anyway.
– Paul McCartney

There are still more ideas buzzing around in the Beatles' heads than in most of the pop world put together . . . They'll never be able to copy this. Neither will the Beatles be able to reproduce a tenth of this material on a live performance. But who cares? Let John, Paul, George and Ringo worry about that when the time comes.
– *Melody Maker*, 1966

TRACK LIST

Side 1:
Taxman (Harrison)
Eleanor Rigby (Lennon-McCartney)
I'm Only Sleeping (Lennon-McCartney)
Love You To (Harrison)
Here, There And Everywhere (Lennon-McCartney)
Yellow Submarine (Lennon-McCartney)
She Said She Said (Lennon-McCartney)

Side 2:

Good Day Sunshine (Lennon-McCartney)
And Your Bird Can Sing (Lennon-McCartney)
For No One (Lennon-McCartney)
Doctor Robert (Lennon-McCartney)
I Want To Tell You (Harrison)
Got To Get You Into My Life (Lennon-McCartney)
Tomorrow Never Knows (Lennon-McCartney)

Released: 5 August 1966 (Parlophone)
Highest chart position: 1
Weeks in chart: 34 (7 at number 1)

FAB FACT

No song from *Revolver* found its way into the set of The Beatles' summer world tour, highlighting how much the band's work in the studio was becoming incompatible with live performance. The recording of the album was the first time the band attended and worked in the mixing sessions.

FAB FACT

'Tomorrow Never Knows', the final song on the album, was the first one recorded by The Beatles in 1966 – and quite the statement of a new direction. After John and George's dental experience, John threw himself into experimenting with LSD. The lyrics of 'Tomorrow Never Knows' were inspired by his reading of Timothy Leary and Richard Alpert's *The Psychedelic Experience*. The song was originally called 'The Void', though John, feeling self-conscious of the lyric, later gave the song its known title – another Ringoism.

FAB FACT

In the studio, John told Martin that he wanted the vocal of 'Tomorrow Never Knows' to sound like the Dalai Lama and 4,000 monks chanting on a mountaintop. To try to accomplish this, John's vocal was fed through a revolving Leslie speaker inside a Hammond organ. To add the distinctive sound effects throughout the song, the band created tape loops on their Brenell tape recorders, feeding the tapes at the right moments during recording. Sounds recorded in these tape loops include Paul laughing, a Mellotron on a flute setting and the guitar solo in 'Taxman'.

FAB FACT

George seems to have found it hard to decide on titles for his songs on the album. During recording, 'Love You To' had the working title of 'Granny Smith', while 'I Want To Tell You' was originally called 'Laxton's Superb', both kinds of apple.

FAB FACT

The horn section in 'Got To Get You Into My Life' includes two of Georgie Fame's Blue Flames: Eddie Thornton and Peter Coe.

FAB FACT

For the first time, the album cover was not by photographer Robert Freeman, though his photographs were featured. Klaus Voormann, The Beatles' old friend from their Hamburg days, was brought in to create the iconic pen-and-ink and photo collage. Klaus was living in London, playing bass for Manfred Mann by then, and had been inspired by the Aubrey Beardsley exhibition that ran at the V & A Museum in 1966.

55

ALL THESE PLACES HAD THEIR MOMENTS

THE BEATLES' THIRD WORLD TOUR

IMELDA STOOD UP: FIRST FAMILY
WAITS IN VAIN FOR MOPHEADS
– Newspaper headline, Manila

After the restful, and then creative, beginning to the year, The Beatles embarked on another summer world tour. Jaded at the prospect, the band didn't fit in time to rehearse, and at their first gig in Germany, Paul forgot the words to 'I'm Down'. Still, the German leg of the tour did provide a special moment when they reunited with their Hamburg pals.

This proved to be the last positive experience on the tour. They flew into Japan amid a swirl of controversy and protest due to their having been invited to play at the Nippon Budokan, considered by many to be a sacred venue purely for the practice and showcasing of martial arts. So troubled were the Japanese authorities by The Beatles, that the band were accompanied by 35,000 security personnel.

Worse was to come when they landed in the Philippines. The band were expected to visit Imelda Marcos for a morning reception at the Malacañang Palace, but there was a miscommunication between the tour promoter and government officials. The Beatles were unaware of the invitation and didn't show up. In the morning, having switched on the television in their hotel room, they watched a live broadcast of the reception, the cameras lingering over disappointed, crying and angry faces.

The Filipino media cried foul, and their visit became increasingly dangerous. Death threats were sent to their hotel and to the British embassy, and Epstein quickly arranged a camera crew to film an apologetic press statement. But on broadcast a mysterious surge of static wiped out the footage. The Beatles and their team decided to leave the country quicksmart. Their security was withdrawn, a tax commissioner told them they couldn't leave without paying taxes on their share of the two shows' takings (despite the promoter having withheld it), and the tax was to be deducted from the promoter's share. Epstein paid up anyway.

They were jostled and kicked as they made their way from the hotel to the airport, where they were left to manhandle all their luggage and equipment. Then the escalators were powered down. Epstein, Mal Evans and Alf Bicknell were pushed, punched and shoved through to the departure lounge, and The Beatles, in a smart – or cowardly – move, depending on your viewpoint, hid behind a group of nuns until they got on the plane.

Before the plane took off, as everyone was taking their seats, Evans and press officer Tony Barrow were called off the plane. Unsure whether they would be allowed to get back on, Evans told George to tell his wife Lil that he loved her. Back in the airport, Filipino officials declared that the plane couldn't leave as there was no administrative record of the band and their entourage's arrival. After much scrabbling around, proof was at last provided and the plane was allowed to take off.

Back in Britain, when a reporter asked George what was next, he replied, 'We're going to have a couple of weeks to recuperate before we go and get beaten up by the Americans.' This comment turned out to be more prescient than he could've known.

56

BIGGER THAN JESUS

God bless America. Thank you, Jesus.
– John Lennon, 1978

In March 1966, as The Beatles were resting before the *Revolver* sessions, John invited journalist Maureen Cleave to his Weybridge home for an interview. They discussed various topics around his fame, career and interests, including religion. John had been reading a lot of books on the subject, and during the interview he said, 'Christianity will go. It will vanish and shrink. I needn't argue about that; I'm right and I will be proved right. We're more popular than Jesus now; I don't know which will go first – rock 'n' roll or Christianity. Jesus was alright but his disciples were thick and ordinary. It's them twisting it that ruins it for me.'

The article was published with no comment in the UK – likewise in the *New York Times*. Then it was syndicated to *Datebook* magazine and published in July, just before The Beatles were due to start their new US tour. Lennon's 'I don't know which will go first – rock 'n' roll or Christianity' was the front page quote, and all hell broke loose.

Radio station WAQY in Birmingham, Alabama, banned all Beatles music and called for public burnings of their records and memorabilia. Twenty-two other radio stations across the country followed suit. The national broadcasting service in South Africa joined in with the ban as did radio stations in Holland and Spain.

The Pope even commented on the furore in the Vatican newspaper *L'Osservatore Romano*.

Epstein weighed up cancelling the US tour, but instead went over to America before the band to hold his own press conference. His objective was to dampen the heat from all sides, but the US media wanted a personal apology from John.

The Beatles flew out to the US on 11 August and held their own press conference in Astor Towers in Chicago. The junket was entirely different to the kind the band were used to, with none of the usual trivial questions on haircuts, girlfriends or Jelly Babies. Instead, a contrite John, while not offering an outright apology, sought to explain and contextualise what he meant by his remarks.

A Beatle burning. *Getty Images*

57

ALL THESE PLACES HAD THEIR MOMENTS

THE LAST US TOUR

John wanted to give up more than the others.
He said that he'd had enough.
– Ringo Starr

Though John had quelled the media furore surrounding his comments, the US tour was plagued by nerve-shredding incidents.

In Cleveland, 2,500 fans invaded the pitch of the city's stadium. In Washington, DC, the Ku Klux Klan demonstrated outside the concert venue. In Memphis, the band received an anonymous phone call warning them of an assassination attempt that would take place during their gig. On their second show in the city, a fan threw a firecracker on stage. In Cincinnati, amid a downpour, the show was postponed for the night as the tour operators had failed to build a canopy above the stage and the band's equipment was sodden. In Los Angeles, the gate from their hotel on to the street was locked, and The Beatles found themselves trapped within their armoured van for two hours, surrounded by fans screaming and pounding the sides of the vehicle.

By the time they reached San Francisco and their last show of the tour at Candlestick Park, The Beatles had decided that they could not go on touring. Nothing was announced, but the band took cameras on stage with them and between songs took pictures of each other and the crowd of 25,000. At the end of the concert, they walked off stage, the screams still ringing in their ears. In the plane heading back to the UK, George announced, 'Well, that's it. I'm not a Beatle any more.'

58

WHAT NEXT FOR THE BEATLES?

At that San Francisco gig it seemed that this could possibly be the last time, but I never felt 100 per cent certain till we got back to London.
— Ringo Starr

Despite being one of the most vocal about ending touring, John had a feeling of panic when the reality of their decision kicked in. So, after The Beatles returned to the UK, John flew off again, with Neil Aspinall, to take part in Richard Lester's latest film project, the satirical black comedy *How I Won the War*. Starring Michael Crawford, Jack MacGowran and Roy Kinnear, the film follows a fictional regiment during the Second World War. John took a supporting role, playing Private Gripweed, a musketeer known for looting. To complete his departure from Beatlemania, John cut his hair short and wore NHS 'granny' spectacles, which he kept after shooting.

On his return from the film shoot, in November 1966, he was invited to a new art exhibition in the Indica Gallery. The work was that of New York conceptual artist Yoko Ono.

Paul was the last to be convinced of the necessity of stopping touring. As John took on the role of Private Gripweed, Paul, also with doubts about the repercussions of their decision, decided to go travelling. In disguise, he drove through France, writing a journal and making short films, experimenting with various

John while filming Richard Lester's *How I Won the War. Alamy*

techniques in distortion and superimposition. After this time on his own, he hooked up with Mal Evans and the pair travelled to Kenya to go on safari. On his return to London, he funded some countercultural projects he was interested in, and worked with Martin on the film score for the Boulting brothers' new film, *The Family Way*, starring John and Hayley Mills. One of their compositions, 'Love In The Open Air', received an Ivor Novello Award in 1967 for Best Song in a Film.

George, the most untroubled about the future, headed off to India with Pattie for six weeks to study the sitar under the tuition of Ravi Shankar and Shambhu Das. He was keen to travel and find out more about Indian society, philosophy and culture. He and Pattie arrived in Bombay, and word soon got out that a Beatle was abroad, threatening to disturb his plans for a more immersive travelling experience. To combat this, he held a press conference where he laid out his intentions with candour, and he remained relatively undisturbed for the rest of the trip, heading up to Kashmir to continue his spiritual studies.

Ringo was the happiest of the four to enjoy a more domesticated break from Beatlemania. Always open to the investment advice he received from The Beatles' accountants, he invested in a (short-lived) company, Brickey Building Co. Ltd, which specialised in property development, building adjustments and interior design. In October, he went out to Spain with Maureen and Cynthia to visit John while he was filming.

Knowing that there was not going to be a traditional Christmas album from The Beatles, EMI put together a greatest hits compilation, *A Collection Of Beatles Oldies . . . But Goldies*. Comprised of The Beatles singles, plus a few extra tracks that had been included on EPs, the album was released on 9 December 1966. It failed to reach the top spot in the chart, peaking at number seven, but stayed in the Top 40 for thirty-four weeks.

59

SONGBOOK

STRAWBERRY FIELDS FOREVER/PENNY LANE

A-side:
Strawberry Fields Forever (Lennon-McCartney)

A-side:
Penny Lane (Lennon-McCartney)

Released: 17 February 1967 (Parlophone)
Highest chart position: 2
Weeks in chart: 11

FAB FACT

With no new releases since *Revolver* in August 1966, and the press wondering if the band had dried up, EMI pushed for a release taken from the recordings The Beatles had been working on since getting back in the studio in November 1966. In the can, earmarked for their next album, were 'Strawberry Fields Forever' and 'Penny Lane'. Released as a double A-side, it was the first Beatles single not to reach the top of the charts, kept off the number one spot by Engelbert Humperdink's ballad, 'Release Me'.

John wrote 'Strawberry Fields Forever' while he was on location filming *How I Won the War*. Tapping into the nostalgia he had explored during the recording of *Rubber Soul*, the song featured Strawberry Fields, the grounds around the Salvation Army children's home close to where he'd lived as a boy. Similarly, Paul first mentioned the song 'Penny Lane' in an interview in 1965, and incorporated the shops (including the barber Bioletti's) and buildings in the Penny Lane area of Liverpool.

The Beatles recorded two versions of 'Strawberry Fields Forever', a light, acoustic version with the Mellotron, percussion instruments, harmonies and some sound effect overdubs, then a full, heavier orchestral version with brass, strings and a new vocal by John. He then decided that he liked the beginning of the first version and the end of the orchestral version. Both versions, however, were recorded in a different key, and a different speed, so Martin ironed out the differences by changing the speed of the two versions and editing them together a minute into the song.

The recording of 'Penny Lane' was nearing its completion when Paul decided it needed an extra ingredient to make it sing. He'd watched David Mason on TV playing the piccolo trumpet as the English Chamber Orchestra played Bach's *Brandenburg Concerto No. 2 in F major* and invited him to Abbey Road. Paul sang the part he wanted Mason to play to Martin, who wrote it out; David then recorded it. He was paid £27/10s (£27.50) for his iconic contribution.

60

SONGBOOK

SGT. PEPPER'S LONELY HEARTS CLUB BAND

A decisive moment in the history of Western civilisation.
– Kenneth Tynan, *The Times*

Sgt. Pepper *for me it's a fine album, it's a fine album,
but I did learn to play chess on it.*
– Ringo Starr

TRACK LIST

Side 1:
Sgt. Pepper's Lonely Hearts Club Band (Lennon-McCartney)
With A Little Help From My Friends (Lennon-McCartney)
Lucy In The Sky With Diamonds (Lennon-McCartney)
Getting Better (Lennon-McCartney)
Fixing A Hole (Lennon-McCartney)
She's Leaving Home (Lennon-McCartney)
Being For The Benefit Of Mr. Kite! (Lennon-McCartney)

Side 2:
Within You Without You (Harrison)
When I'm Sixty-Four (Lennon-McCartney)
Lovely Rita (Lennon-McCartney)

Good Morning, Good Morning (Lennon-McCartney)
Sgt. Pepper's Lonely Hearts Club Band (*Reprise*) (Lennon-McCartney)
A Day In The Life (Lennon-McCartney)

Released: 1 June 1967 (Parlophone)
Highest chart position: 1
Weeks in chart: 256 (28 at number 1)

FAB FACT

Paul came up with the idea of an alter-ego band on the flight back from his trip to Africa, using the influence of psychedelic bands such as Big Brother and the Holding Company and the Bonzo Dog Doo-Dah Band. Mal Evans and Paul started riffing during the in-flight dinner, and *Sgt. Pepper* was born.

FAB FACT

The album's closing masterpiece, 'A Day In The Life', was one of John and Paul's most outstanding collaborations. John wrote his verses at the piano with the *Daily Mail* newspaper of 17 January

The Beatles recording *Sgt. Pepper* in Abbey Road studios. *Alamy*

1967 in front of him. It carried the story of the coroner's verdict on the death of the Guinness heir Tara Browne (who first gave Paul LSD), who had run a red light while speeding in his Lotus Elan and crashed into a parked lorry, as well as one on a council survey in Blackburn that reported 4,000 holes in the town's roads.

Paul had the morning routine fragment, and he and John decided that they should fit the two pieces of music together. Paul added the refrain 'I'd love to turn you on' to John's verses, and while unsure of what would go in between, Evans was recorded counting twenty-four bars then setting off an alarm clock. The 'musical orgasm' that then filled these bars was also Paul's idea.

FAB FACT

The orchestral crescendo in 'A Day In The Life' was filmed on 16mm film during a special party session on Friday, 10 February 1967. Those present included Brian Jones, Mick Jagger, Keith Richards, Marianne Faithfull, Pattie Harrison, Graham Nash, Donovan, Mike Nesmith from The Monkees, and art collective The Fool (who arrived dressed as tarot cards). The orchestra were there in full evening dress and joke accessories such as false noses, bald caps, fake glasses, moustaches and nipples, as well as streamers, bubbles and party hats. John told Martin he wanted the noise in the twenty-four bars to sound like 'the end of the world', while Paul made the less abstract suggestion that each player start playing quietly on their instrument's lowest note, ending as loudly as possible on their instrument's highest note, and to get there, in the bars in between, as randomly as possible. Both Martin and Paul conducted the orchestra, Paul noting that the string players tended to follow each other, while the brass players were more comfortable with improvisation. The film of the evening was never broadcast, though snippets of the session were shown in the *Beatles Anthology* documentary.

The Beatles chat through *Pepper* ideas with George Martin. *Alamy*

FAB FACT

George Martin's experience with sound effects was used with great success in a number of songs on the album: the audience laughter in the title song was taken from a live recording of *Beyond the Fringe*; in 'Good Morning, Good Morning', he added the animal and hunting sounds, though it was John who instructed him to put them in the order of how each animal could be eaten by its successor; in 'Being For The Benefit Of Mr. Kite!', with another brilliantly abstract instruction from John – 'I want to smell the sawdust' – Martin gathered together tape of calliope pieces and other fairground noises, had engineer Geoff Emerick throw them up in the air, and then reassembled them in random order; and between the final chord of 'A Day In The Life' (made by John, Paul, Ringo, Martin and Evans all pounding an E major chord on three pianos) and the gibberish on the run-out groove (many fans got in touch to say if you played that small section backwards it sounded like The Beatles shouting 'We fuck like Superman') is a high-pitched whistle that only dogs can hear.

Pop artist Peter Blake created the album cover, on the recommendation of art dealer Robert Fraser, after a conversation with Paul who was brainstorming his ideas of a wall of fame and a mood of municipal gardens and military bands. Each Beatle was asked to come up with a list of heroes to include on the cover: John suggested Oscar Wilde, Edgar Allan Poe and Lewis Carroll, who all appeared on the finished cover, as well as Jesus and Adolf Hitler, who did not; Paul's suggestions included William Burroughs and Fred Astaire; George suggested various Indian gurus such as Mahavatar Babaji and Paramahansa Yogananda; and Ringo was happy to go along with everyone else's suggestions. Mahatma Gandhi was to appear on the cover, but that was vetoed by Sir Joseph Lockwood, Head of EMI, who thought it would be too controversial in India. The photograph was taken by Michael Cooper at his studio on 30 March 1967.

Once the final acetate was ready, Paul took it to Mama Cass's house in Chelsea and blasted the album out into the street as the sun rose, much to the neighbours' delight; they appeared bleary-eyed but applauding at their doors. On release, the album shot straight to the top of the chart, and became the biggest-selling album of all time until it was toppled by Michael Jackson's *Thriller* in 1982. And although the album quickly achieved legendary status, not everyone was a fan: the BBC banned 'A Day In The Life' and 'Lucy In The Sky With Diamonds' for 'promoting drug use'. Contrary to belief at the time, 'Lucy In The Sky With Diamonds' was named after a drawing done by John's son, Julian, and had nothing to do with LSD.

61

SONGBOOK

ALL YOU NEED IS LOVE/BABY, YOU'RE A RICH MAN

A-side:
All You Need Is Love (Lennon-McCartney)

B-side:
Baby, You're A Rich Man (Lennon-McCartney)

Released: 7 July 1967 (Parlophone)
Highest chart position: 1
Weeks in chart: 13 (3 at number 1)

FAB FACT

'Our World', the first-ever live satellite broadcast linking up twenty-four countries all over the world, was broadcast on 25 June 1967. Each country taking part was to air something that represented the culture of the nation, and the UK decided on The Beatles recording their next single, 'All You Need Is Love'. A total of 150 million people across the globe watched the broadcast.

FAB FACT

The Beatles rehearsed and recorded the song over five days before 'Our World', but the vocals, Paul's bass, George's guitar solo, Ringo's drums and the orchestra were recorded live on the day. Just as when they recorded the orchestral 'orgasm' on *Sgt. Pepper*'s 'A Day In The Life', friends including Mick Jagger, Keith Richards, Marianne Faithfull, Pattie Harrison, Graham Nash, Hunter Davies, Mike McCartney, Keith Moon, Jane Asher and Eric Clapton were invited to come along to the 'Our World' session.

FAB FACT

In the fadeout, The Beatles had fun with their own history, gleefully singing out, 'She loves you, yeah, yeah, yeah'. The orchestra joined in, playing sections of 'Greensleeves' and Glenn Miller's 'In The Mood'. The latter song, unfortunately, was still in copyright, and The Beatles had to make an out-of-court settlement to the publishers.

62

R.I.P. BRIAN EPSTEIN

A terrible and stupid accident.
– business colleague Don Black

When The Beatles stopped touring in 1966, many in Epstein's team worried that he would find his role in looking after his boys diminished. He visited the studio infrequently so his involvement with *Sgt. Pepper* was minor, but in other areas of Beatles business he was still as involved as ever: negotiating a new contract for them with EMI, supporting Paul after his drug revelations in the media, and putting together a full-page advert in *The Times* supporting the legalisation of marijuana on behalf of the band.

He was also putting into place changes at NEMS, the business that held a management share in the band, so he could concentrate on other projects. He brought in another impresario, Robert Stigwood, to become his joint managing director, although he continued to manage the careers of The Beatles and his other favourite act, Cilla Black. He had leased the Saville Theatre in 1965 to put on various plays and revues, and even directed a play himself, *A Smashing Day*. His many trips to Spain led him to finance a film on bull fighting, and in the weeks leading up to his death, he was excited about a trip to Canada and America to compere a televised variety spectacular.

Yet his mood swings dogged him. He was heavily reliant on drugs to get him up through the day and then down to sleep at night. And in July 1967, his father died. His mother visited him

Ringo, George and John speak to the press after they
have just been informed of Brian Epstein's death. *Getty Images*

in early August, and plans were put in place for her to move down
to London permanently.

On the August bank holiday weekend, as The Beatles headed to
Bangor to study under the Maharishi Mahesh Yogi, Epstein was
looking forward to hosting a party at his country house in Sussex.
Friends and colleagues Peter Brown and Geoffrey Ellis arrived in
the evening without the friends they said they were going to bring
along, and he was disappointed. Looking for a party, he headed
back to London, saying he would be back later that weekend.

By Sunday, he had still not returned. When the butler in his
London flat knocked on his bedroom door to get him up, there
was no answer. The housekeeper made some phone calls around his
friends, and eventually a local doctor forced the bedroom door open.

Brian Epstein's death was front page news. The Beatles,
devastated, cut short their Bangor trip. Out of respect to the
family and so the service could be a private affair, they didn't
attend his funeral. The coroner's verdict was death by accidental
overdose of barbiturates and alcohol. He was thirty-two years old.

63

SONGBOOK

HELLO, GOODBYE/I AM THE WALRUS

A-side:
Hello, Goodbye (Lennon-McCartney)

B-side:
I Am The Walrus (Lennon-McCartney)

Released: 24 November 1967 (Parlophone)
Highest chart position: 1
Weeks in chart: 12 (7 at number 1)

FAB FACT

'Hello, Goodbye' was composed as an experiment into 'the random' with Paul playing word association games with the band's assistant, Alistair Taylor.

FAB FACT

John wrote 'I Am The Walrus' after childhood friend Pete Shotton told him that back in the English classes at Quarry Bank High School teachers were analysing the lyrics of his songs 'Strawberry Fields Forever' and 'Tomorrow Never Knows'. He later said that he deliberately wrote a meaningless nonsense lyric in reply.

FAB FACT

The melody for 'I Am The Walrus' came to John while he was at his piano and heard a police siren in the background. He was angry that 'I Am The Walrus' was relegated to the B-side. Still, the single went on to become the biggest-selling Beatles record since 'She Loves You'.

FAB FACT

The BBC banned airplay of 'I Am The Walrus' due to the lyric 'Boy, you've been a naughty girl, you let your knickers down.'

64

SONGBOOK

MAGICAL MYSTERY TOUR (FILM SOUNDTRACK)

They lost the plot with their dopey TV film, but 1967 was still their zenith as songwriters. For once, the U.S. release went better than the British original . . . The result was simply the best set of Beatles tunes so far on a single disc.
– Paul Du Noyer, *Blender*

This is The Beatles out there in front and the rest of us in their wake.
– Nick Logan, *NME*

TRACK LIST

Side 1:
Magical Mystery Tour (Lennon-McCartney)
The Fool On The Hill (Lennon-McCartney)
Flying (Lennon-McCartney-Harrison-Starkey)
Blue Jay Way (Harrison)
Your Mother Should Know (Lennon-McCartney)
I Am The Walrus (Lennon-McCartney)

Side 2:
Hello, Goodbye (Lennon-McCartney)
Strawberry Fields Forever (Lennon-McCartney)

Penny Lane (Lennon-McCartney)
Baby, You're A Rich Man (Lennon-McCartney)
All You Need Is Love (Lennon-McCartney)

EP
Released: 8 December 1967 (Parlophone)
Highest chart position: 2
Weeks in chart: 12

FAB FACT

The Beatles started recording the songs for *Magical Mystery Tour* only four days after they finished *Sgt. Pepper's Lonely Hearts Club Band*. Paul got the idea for the film after he visited Jane Asher in the US. He came across Ken Kesey and his Merry Pranksters on their psychedelic painted bus and thought The Beatles could come up with their own version.

FAB FACT

Magical Mystery Tour was first released as a double EP in the UK, with the tracklist made up of the songs included in the film. It was kept off the number one spot by the single 'Hello, Goodbye'. It was Capitol in the US that added the 1967 singles and released it as a full album. The full album was released in the UK for the first time in 1976, though the US import appeared in the UK Top forty in early 1968.

FAB FACT

Brian Epstein's last visit to a recording session was while The Beatles were recording 'Your Mother Should Know' in Chappell Studios, London.

FAB FACT

Magical Mystery Tour contains the only song credited to Lennon-McCartney-Harrison-Starkey. 'Flying' is an instrumental (the original title was 'Aerial Tour Instrumental'), and it was used in the film over scenes of cloudy Arctic landscapes taken from Stanley Kubrick's *Dr. Strangelove* outtakes.

65

ON THE SILVER SCREEN

MAGICAL MYSTERY TOUR

The Beatles' Magical Mystery Tour is superb, brilliant, great, heavy, boss, light entertainment, good clean fun, a Message Picture, an entertaining nightmare, and it has good rock and roll music. It is by far the best of the Beatle films. It is not what you expect it to be at all.
– Tom Nolan, *Los Angeles Free Press*

When the show was screened by the BBC on December 26, the switchboard at the TV company's London headquarters was jammed with calls from baffled viewers who didn't understand what Magical Mystery Tour was all about.
– Tony Barrow, *KRLA Beat* magazine

Four days after Epstein's death, The Beatles met in Paul's house in St John's Wood to discuss what they would do next. They had vetoed Robert Stigwood becoming their manager, but decided to stay with NEMS under the silent care of Epstein's brother, Clive. They also decided to crack on with filming their television film, *Magical Mystery Tour*, now that they had six soundtrack songs recorded.

Before he died, Epstein had been positive about the project, going over Paul's script – famously a big circle on a piece of paper divided into scene sections like a pie chart – to make sure all the band members were equally represented and taking notes on pre-production issues. He'd also booked cinematographer Peter Theobald, but otherwise the production was completely in the hands of The Beatles.

Armed with their pie chart and a copy of *Spotlight*, the theatre trade magazine, The Beatles began casting the film: Jessie Robbins was to play Ringo's aunt; Derek Royle, the courier Jolly Jimmy Johnson; and Mandy Weet was the glamorous tour hostess Wendy Winters. Paul was a fan of Ivor Cutler, so cast him as the bus conductor, Buster Bloodvessel, and John recruited variety star Nat Jackley.

On 11 September, the cast, some friends, a crew of four cameramen, a sound man and a technical adviser climbed aboard the bus at Allsop Place in London. Off they went on their merry way, travelling and filming in Devon, Cornwall and Somerset.

The Beatles on the bus for their *Magical Mystery Tour*. Alamy

It was a chaotic yet good-natured shoot. Paul took on most of the directing responsibilities but everyone chipped in with ideas, and some highlights came about by chance. The 'Jessie's Dream' sequence of John as a waiter shovelling spaghetti on to Aunt Jess's plate was added after John told Paul of a dream he'd had. Naively, The Beatles didn't realise that you had to book studios in advance, but they did manage to film some scenes at RAF West Malling, including the impressive Busby Berkeley-inspired performance of 'Your Mother Should Know'. Victor Spinetti, the Beatles favourite who starred in *A Hard Day's Night* and *Help!*, reprised his role in Joan Littlewood's stage musical *Oh! What a Lovely War*, the Bonzo Dog Doo-Dah Band did a star turn in the strip-show scene, and Paul even managed a trip to the south of France to film his 'Fool On The Hill' section.

The band's naivety became evident in the editing suite where they discovered that, because they hadn't used clapper boards, the sound in each of the musical numbers was out of sync. But, undaunted, sharing the editing duties with Roy Benson, they managed to shape ten hours of material into their fifty-three-minute film, ready for broadcast in the BBC's prime Boxing Day evening slot.

The TV critics hated it. *Magical Mystery Tour* was slated as the first major failure of the Fab Four. Paul stoutly defended the film, pointing out that it hadn't helped that it had been shown in black and white, and that 'the Queen's speech was hardly a gas'.

66

SONGBOOK

LADY MADONNA/THE INNER LIGHT

A-side:
Lady Madonna (Lennon-McCartney)

B-side:
The Inner Light (Harrison)

Released: 15 March 1968 (Parlophone)
Highest chart position: 1
Weeks in chart: 8 (2 at number 1)

FAB FACT

'Lady Madonna' was recorded in a single day in February 1968 before the band headed off to Rishikesh to meditate with the Maharishi Mahesh Yogi. It was the last Beatles single to be released by Parlophone; every album and single after this was released on their own label, Apple.

FAB FACT

Paul was inspired to write the song after seeing a picture in a *National Geographic* magazine of a Malayo-Polynesian woman suckling her baby with two other children around her.

George recorded the instrumental track for 'The Inner Light' in EMI's studios in Mumbai, India, when he was producing the soundtrack for the spaced-out psychedelic thriller *Wonderwall*, starring Jane Birkin and Jack MacGowran. He was inspired to write the song after reading the *Tao Te Ching*.

The Beatles made a video to promote 'Lady Madonna' while they were in India. The footage is of them recording the song 'Hey Bulldog', later used in the *Yellow Submarine* soundtrack.

67

THE FIFTH BEATLE

MAHARISHI MAHESH YOGI

*I will never forget the dedication that he wrote
inside a book he once gave me, which read
'radiate bliss consciousness', and that to me says it all.*
– Paul McCartney

The Maharishi came into The Beatles' orbit in 1967. He'd been recommended by Pattie Harrison, who had joined the Spiritual Regeneration Movement after her trip to India in 1966 with George. When she heard that the Maharishi was to give a lecture in the Hilton Hotel in London, she told George. He invited the rest of the band. Ringo couldn't attend as Maureen had just had their second child, Jason, but she encouraged Ringo to join the rest of the band at the Maharishi's weekend retreat in Bangor. It was there that they learned of Epstein's death. The Beatles decided to visit his meditation retreat in Rishikesh, India, in early 1968 to immerse themselves in his teachings.

The exact birth date of the Maharishi is unknown (he dismissed birthdays as irrelevant), but it is most likely that he was born on 12 January 1918. He was born Mahesh Prasad Varma, in Jabalpur, into the high-status Kayastha caste – those who specialise in the fields of administration, politics and writing legal and historical documents.

The Beatles gather round Maharishi Mahesh Yogi to hear his teachings on Transcendental Meditation. *Alamy*

After attaining a degree in physics at the Allahabad University, he became a disciple and then secretary to Swami Brahmananda Saraswati (also known as Guru Dev), the spiritual leader of the Joshimath region in the Himalayas. The men worked together until Guru Dev's death in 1953. The Maharishi then spent two years in recluse before announcing, in 1955, that he would take the teaching of transcendental meditation (TM) across India, and then out into the world. He now called himself Maharishi ('Great Sage').

By 1967, he had given countless lectures, published books and opened 250 TM centres around the world. His association with The Beatles was to bring him and his cause great fame (and money).

Dogged by the Indian tax authorities, he set up his global TM headquarters in Switzerland, then the Netherlands, while continuing to travel the globe. In 1992, he inaugurated the Natural Law Party (NLP), which was active in forty-two different countries, and reconnected with George, who generously supported the NLP with a benefit concert in the Royal Albert Hall. In the UK General Election that year, every NLP candidate lost their deposit. By the late nineties, the Maharishi had stopped appearing in public due to poor health, though he continued to write and communicate with his followers via CCTV. He died peacefully in his sleep, in Limburg, in 2008.

68

ALL THESE PLACES HAD THEIR MOMENTS

RISHIKESH

*John kept saying, 'I'm here because of George.' George was
the real McCoy. He was a real seeker. He was what he
was whether he was a Beatle or not.*
– Prudence Farrow

Rishikesh is a city located around 200 miles north of Delhi in the Himalayan foothills. In this area of great natural beauty, the Maharishi's ashram sat in secluded, private grounds where monkeys, parrots and peacocks were free to roam around. The accommodation consisted of simple, comfortable bungalows, as well as a lecture hall and dining area. A staff of forty, including cooks, gardeners, cleaners and even a masseuse tended to the guests' needs.

George, Pattie, her sister Jenny, John and Cynthia, and Mal Evans arrived at the retreat first, followed later by Paul and Jane, Ringo and Maureen. Also in residence were Mike Love from the Beach Boys, Donovan, his friend Cosmic Dave, Mia Farrow and her sister, Prudence – who became the inspiration behind one of the most beautiful songs on The Beatles' next album.

The residents could take part in TM workshops and lectures, practise meditation themselves, and share their experiences at the communal meals. There was plenty of free time to sunbathe, walk the grounds, visit other local towns, and, of course, write songs. The Beatles were hugely prolific during their stay, and, inspired by their fellow residents – Donovan taught John his finger-picking guitar-playing technique and Mike Love helped Paul with 'Back In The USSR' – wrote around forty songs that would find themselves on the White Album and *Abbey Road*.

One night, the whole camp took part in a torchlight procession to a boat on the Ganges, where they spent the night singing and dancing. Another time, the Maharishi offered a trip in his helicopter to one of the residents, and John convinced the Maharishi that it should be him. Afterwards, when Paul asked him why he was so keen on the helicopter trip – he had been in

George, Ringo and Pattie Boyd at the Maharishi
Mahesh Yogi's ashram in Rishikesh,1968. *Alamy*

helicopters before – John replied that he thought the Maharishi might 'slip him the answer'.

Ringo and Maureen stayed for two weeks, but they missed their children and Maureen hated the flies. Although they'd arrived with a suitcase of baked beans, and Mal Evans secured a steady supply of eggs, Ringo's sensitive stomach couldn't take the spicy vegetarian food.

Paul and Jane left after a month, both getting what they wanted from the trip, while John and George intended to stay for the full three months. A couple of weeks after Paul left, a rumour flew around the camp that the Maharishi had made a pass at Mia Farrow. It was never confirmed by her, and was possibly started by Magic Alex, a Beatles acolyte who was particularly friendly with John and envious of the Maharishi's influence on his friend. John, already losing faith and suspicious of the Maharishi's motives, decided to leave, particularly when George said he was departing to carry on with his travels to southern India. When the Maharishi asked why they weren't staying longer, John replied, 'If you're so fucking cosmic, you'll know why.'

In the taxi on the way to the airport, John started to compose a critical song about the Maharishi, though when George told him the lyrics were a bit unfair, he changed the song's character from 'Maharishi' to 'Sexy Sadie'.

69

THE FIFTH BEATLE

YOKO ONO

*I was a working-class macho guy who was
used to being served and Yoko didn't buy that.*
– John Lennon

Yoko Ono was born in Tokyo, Japan, on 18 February 1933. Her mother belonged to the wealthy Yasuda banking family, and her dad, although from an artistic family and a talented classical pianist, worked for the Yokohama Specie Bank. Yet, despite her privileged background, Yoko's childhood was often lonely, her governess her most constant companion, and she would often retreat into her imagination.

During the Second World War, with her dad interned in a camp in Hanoi, she was sent to the relative safety of the countryside with her younger brother and sister. Often hungry and forced to barter for food (often unsuccessfully) with their city possessions – Yoko would describe sumptuous menus to her younger siblings as a distraction.

Japan's economy recovered rapidly after the war, and life for Yoko resumed. She attended the exclusive Gakashūin School. She was a talented pianist, gifted at languages, literature and the visual arts, and when she enrolled at the Gakashūin University, it was as the first-ever female student of philosophy.

A two-year-old Yoko Ono poses with her
mother, Isoko, and father, Eisuke. *Getty Images*

When Yoko was eighteen, her dad, now president of the Bank of Tokyo, was transferred to New York, and the family set up home in Scarsdale, Connecticut. Yoko joined the liberal, all-women Sarah Lawrence College to carry on her studies in philosophy, literature and music, but her rebellious, questioning nature was soon too much for her teachers. She received a marriage proposal from one of Japan's wealthiest men, much to the relief of her family, but rather than accepting, Yoko dropped out of college, eloped with composer Toshi Ichiyanagi, and found herself in a basic loft apartment in Downtown New York, moving amongst the bohemian set.

She gravitated towards the Fluxus group, a collective of artists, composers, designers, dancers and poets influenced by Dadaist philosophy and headed by George Maciunas. The Fluxus group – experimental, anti-commercial, anti-art – hosted 'happenings', often in venues not associated with culture, to encourage audience participation and shatter the imagined boundaries between art and life. Yoko used sculpture, film and performance to provoke and play with her audiences. One of her most famous pieces was *Cut Piece*, performed in Japan and New York's Carnegie Hall, where she sat on stage fully clothed and invited audience members to come up and cut off a piece of her clothing until she was left naked. She also published her first book, *Grapefruit*, which was full of 'instructional poems' – some whimsical, some spiritual, some cheeky – such as 'Draw a map to get lost' and 'Listen to the sound of the earth turning'.

When her marriage to Ichiyanagi faltered, she took her work to Japan where she received vicious criticism. At this difficult time, she was hospitalised for depression. Fellow artist and fan of her work, Anthony Cox, helped her to recover, and, in 1964, they married. The couple had a daughter, Kyoko Chan. Their relationship was a volatile one, but they stayed together to help each other as artists.

In 1966, Yoko was invited to London to take part in a symposium on 'The Destruction of Art'. When the owner of the Indica Gallery, John Dunbar, heard Yoko was in town, he offered her an exhibition. The day before 'Unfinished Paintings and Objects' was open to the public, Dunbar brought John in for an exclusive viewing. Yoko was displeased at having her attention taken away from her preparations, but introduced herself to

John by giving him a card with the instruction 'Breathe' on it. As John walked round the exhibition, he changed his mind from thinking that the work was a joke to understanding its humour and warmth. He and Yoko met again at her *Painting to Hammer a Nail* artwork, and he asked if he could hammer a nail in. Yoko was reticent – she wanted the board to be pristine for the opening – but Dunbar convinced her to let John do it for a fee. She asked for five shillings. John replied that if he gave her an imaginary five shillings, he would hammer in an imaginary nail. At this moment, a connection was made; she realised that he understood.

They met again briefly at a Claes Oldenburg exhibition, then she sent him a copy of *Grapefruit*, which John loved. They started corresponding, and John backed another of her exhibitions, the 'Half-a Wind Show'. She continued to send him postcards while he was in Rishikesh, and when Cynthia went on holiday to Greece after she and John returned from India, John invited Yoko to Weybridge.

Nervous with each other, they spent the night making the sound collages that would end up as their *Two Virgins* album, released later that year with full-frontal nude cover art. At dawn, they made love – their future together was sealed.

70

APPLE CORPS

Clive Epstein or some other such business freak came up
to us and said, 'You got to spend so much money or
the tax'll take it. We're thinking of opening a chain
of retail clothes,' or some barmy thing like that.
– John Lennon

Epstein's strength in managing The Beatles was in presenting and promoting the Fab Four to the world. By the time of his death, John, Paul, George and Ringo were very wealthy men indeed – the new deal he had brokered with EMI in 1967 having ensured that the record company released £2 million in back royalties to the band. Where his business acumen was less assured was in investment and tax management, and after his death, the accountants were keen to make the most of the money The Beatles had earned.

Apple Publishing came first, headed by Beatles friend and confidant, Terry Doran, to take care of their music publishing portfolio. Then, inspired by Barbara Hulanicki's Biba store, plans were put in place to open an Apple Boutique at 94 Baker Street, to be managed by Pete Shotton, selling clothes, furnishings and other lifestyle products to be designed by Anglo-Dutch art collective, The Fool. Paul described the ethos of the store as 'a beautiful place for beautiful people to buy beautiful things'. By mid-1968, driven by the burgeoning independent, countercultural scene, Apple Corps expanded to invest in film, music and electronics.

Apple took its name from the René Magritte painting *Le jeu de mourre*, gifted to Paul by Robert Fraser to signify the freshness of the new venture. The logo was designed by Gene Mahon from a photograph by Paul Castell. The identity was completed by Alan Aldridge, who drew the copyright lettering to adorn each Apple release.

The Beatles kept a familiar, close-knit team around them to head up each division. Denis O'Dell, assisted by Tony Bramwell, was put in charge of Apple Film. Apple Electronics was led by 'Magic' Alex Mardas. His only real experience of electronics was in television repair, yet he excited The Beatles – John in particular – with his ideas for electronic inventions such as wallpaper with speakers, electrical paint and a solar-powered guitar. He also promised to build a seventy-two-track studio in the basement of the Apple offices. Ron Kass, Head of Liberty Records International, was poached to take charge of Apple Records, with Peter Asher as Head of A&R, whose first job was to bring in singer-songwriter James Taylor.

Heading the whole operation was Managing Director Neil Aspinall, with Alistair Taylor and Peter Brown from NEMS as Office Manager and PA to The Beatles. Mal Evans kept his role as PA to the band. Derek Taylor, who had served as the band's press secretary from 1964 to 1965, was brought back from the US to run Apple's press office. He soon became the public face of Apple, offering generous hospitality to the office's visitors – musicians, film stars, journalists and other industry insiders, not to mention all the dreamers and schemers taking advantage of Apple's open-door policy.

Apple Records was officially launched at a press conference given by John and Paul, accompanied by Neil Aspinall and Magic

Alex, in New York in May 1968. A simultaneous press campaign invited artists of all mediums to send their pitches to the Apple team. The office was inundated with letters, tapes, manuscripts, films and artworks.

The Beatles themselves brought in great talent. Paul, after a conversation over dinner with Twiggy, signed the winner of television's *Opportunity Knocks*, seventeen-year-old Welsh singer Mary Hopkin, who scored a number one hit with her debut single 'Those Were The Days'. Paul went on to write her second single 'Goodbye' and produce her first album, *Postcard*. George signed up and produced Jackie Lomax and, later, Billy Preston, while Ringo brought in classical composer John Tavener. His first album, *The Whale*, was released by Apple.

71

THE FIFTH BEATLE

DEREK TAYLOR

*The Liverpool sound came to Manchester last night and I thought
it was magnificent . . . Indecipherable, meaningless nonsense, of
course, but as beneficial and invigorating as a week on the bench of
the pierhead overlooking the Mersey.*
— Derek Taylor, after seeing The Beatles for the first time

Derek Taylor was born on 7 May 1932 in the Wirral. He left school
at seventeen and joined the local newspaper, *The Hoylake and West
Kirby Advertiser*. Soon, he was writing for the *Liverpool Daily Post*
and *Echo*, and then he was made the northern correspondent for
national newspapers, the *News Chronicle*, *Sunday Dispatch* and
the *Sunday Express*.

In 1962, he became a columnist and theatre critic for the *Daily
Express*, and in May 1963, they sent him to cover The Beatles
and Roy Orbison at the Manchester Odeon, expecting him to
write a sniffy response to these four young upstarts who had been
turning heads. Instead, he offered fulsome praise, understanding
right away that The Beatles were more than a flash-in-the-pan
pop combo – they were big news.

His editors suggested he write a ghosted column by one of
them, and he and George collaborated. Taylor proved himself
such a good fit with the group that Epstein lured him away from

journalism to become his own PA and The Beatles' press secretary, and to ghostwrite his own memoir, *A Cellarful of Noise*.

After a blazing row with Epstein – on the last night of the 1964 US tour, Taylor borrowed Epstein's limousine, leaving Epstein stranded at the Paramount Theatre – he resigned. The following year, he moved with his family to Los Angeles where he worked as a publicist for various American groups, including The Beach Boys, The Byrds, Paul Revere & The Raiders, Captain Beefheart and The Mamas & The Papas. He also helped to organise and publicise the Monterey Pop Festival in the summer of 1967.

Derek Taylor in the Apple offices in his famous wicker chair. *Getty Images*

Despite his fallout with Epstein, he stayed in touch with The Beatles, and when George and Pattie visited California, Taylor accompanied them on their trip to Haight-Ashbury. (George wrote 'Blue Jay Way', which appeared on *Magical Mystery Tour*, while waiting for Taylor on a foggy LA day.)

With his star on the rise, his bulging little black book, and as someone who carried out his promotional duties with charm, flair and imagination, Taylor was the ideal candidate to manage the press team at Apple. At George's suggestion, he returned from sunny LA to take his place at 3 Savile Row in his grand white wicker chair.

After announcing The Beatles' split, Taylor wrote his first memoir, *As Time Goes By*, while continuing to work within the music industry for a variety of clients. He was appointed Director of Special Projects at Warner Bros., eventually becoming Vice-President of Marketing for the company. In the eighties, he returned to writing, working on George's memoir *I · Me · Mine*, Michelle Phillips' autobiography *California Dreamin'* and books based on his own life and times with The Beatles. He also worked with George for Handmade Films, and returned to Apple in the nineties to work on the *Live at the BBC* promotional campaign and the *Anthology* project. He died of cancer in 1997. Paul described him as 'a beautiful man'. He was a true believer in The Beatles' magic, and The Beatles were lucky to have him on their team.

72

ON THE SILVER SCREEN

YELLOW SUBMARINE

*Visually, every conceivable style is thrown in pell-mell:
there is Art Nouveau and psychedelic, op and pop,
dada and surrealist, Hieronymus Bosch and just plain bosh.
Why does it work? Because of its reckless generosity.*
– John Simon, *Film 68/69*

I liked the film. I think it's a classic.
– George Harrison

After *Help!* The Beatles owed United Artists one more film, but
they were less than enthusiastic about the task. Fortunately, in
early 1967, Epstein was approached by Al Brodax, producer of
the American cartoon show *The Beatles*, who wanted to make a
full-length animated film. Epstein and United Artists approved
the idea, but, again, The Beatles were not keen. United Artists
agreed that the characters could be voiced by actors if The Beatles
agreed to provide songs for the soundtrack and film a short guest
appearance. The Beatles agreed and filmed their good-humoured
appearance on 25 January 1968 before they flew out to India.

Meanwhile, director George Dunning brought in Heinz
Edelmann as the film's art director, basing his decision on only a
handful of sketches. Edelmann and Dunning's concepts matched:
the film should move away from the traditional Disney style

of animation and take inspiration from Pop Art. Edelmann structured the film around interconnected shorts, using a variety of styles and techniques that mixed photography and animation to create a wonderfully colourful, kaleidoscopic visual identity, underpinned by The Beatles' music. To fulfil Edelmann's vision forty animators and 140 technical artists were employed, and they completed the film in just eleven months.

The script, which went through fourteen drafts, was written by Lee Minoff, Al Brodax, Jack Mendelsohn and Erich (*Love Story*) Segal. It tells the story of the magical Pepperland under siege by the music-hating Blue Meanies, and how Old Fred recruits The Beatles to help restore music, love, colour and happiness. Liverpool poet Roger McGough, in an uncredited role, was brought in to make the dialogue more Beatley and Liverpudlian.

The characters of The Beatles played along familiar lines. John, voiced by John Clive, was the intellectual; Paul, voiced by Geoffrey Hughes, was the confident showman; George, voiced by Peter Batten, was the mystical philosopher; and Ringo, voiced by Paul Angelis, was the melancholy, kind-hearted everyman. Comedian and impersonator Dick Emery also took part, voicing the characters of the Lord Mayor, Max, the sycophantic Blue Meanie and the Nowhere Man, Jeremy Hillary Boob, PhD.

Yellow Submarine premiered at London's Pavilion Theatre on 17 July 1968, and later in the US in November. The film garnered much critical acclaim, winning a special award at the New York Film Critics Circle award ceremony and being nominated for Best Score at the Grammys. Its release across the UK was hampered by the decision to give it limited distribution across the country's cinemas, so it wasn't a commercial success – it performed better at the box office in the US – but over the years it became a joyful rite of passage for children as an introduction to The Beatles, and a merchandising phenomenon.

73

SONGBOOK

HEY JUDE/REVOLUTION

It might be the first record I ever listened to . . .
I remember that night, laying in my sleeping bag and
singing along to the na-na-na's at the end of the song.
– Dave Grohl on 'Hey Jude'

A-side:
Hey Jude (Lennon-McCartney)

B-side:
Revolution (Lennon-McCartney)

Released: 30 August 1968 (Apple)
Highest chart position: 1
Weeks in chart: 19 (2 at number 1)

FAB FACT

Paul composed 'Hey Jude' as he was driving to Weybridge to comfort Cynthia and Julian Lennon, soon after John had left the family to live with Yoko. The song started as 'Hey Jules', but was changed to 'Jude' because Paul liked the name of the brooding farmhand Jud Fry in the film *Oklahoma!*

FAB FACT

Julian bought the song's recording notes in auction in 1996 for £25,000.

FAB FACT

In March 2020, in California, Paul's handwritten lyrics for 'Hey Jude' sold for £731,000 in auction.

FAB FACT

'Hey Jude' was the first release from Apple Records, and the most successful debut song from an independent label. It was knocked off the top spot in the UK by Apple's second release, the McCartney-produced 'Those Were The Days' by Mary Hopkin. 'Hey Jude' was even more successful in America where it topped the chart for nine weeks – the longest chart-topping run in the US for any Beatles single – and sold six million copies by the end of 1968. The song reached number one in eleven different countries.

FAB FACT

Though The Beatles started the year in the tranquil surroundings of Rishikesh, 1968 was a year of violence and political unrest. John started writing 'Revolution' while in India, demoed it with other Rishikesh compositions at the end of May, and worked on its recording throughout June and July. During this time, he was aware of the Tet Offensive and Mai Lai massacre in Vietnam, the assassinations of Martin Luther King and Robert F. Kennedy, the escalating tension between the USSR and Czechoslovakia, the shooting of Andy Warhol and bloody riots in Paris, London and, later, Chicago. The song was originally earmarked as the next Beatles single, but this was vetoed by Paul and George. They deemed it too slow for a single (the original, laid-back version later featured on the White Album). By the time The Beatles had recorded the faster, more raucous version, Paul had brought in 'Hey Jude'.

The lyrics for 'Revolution' show Lennon's ambivalence towards political revolution, and he agonised over the lyric: 'Don't you know that you can count me out.' In the White Album version, and in some performances, he would replace 'out' with 'in'. This ambivalence was criticised by many on the left at the time as a decadent viewpoint, and Nina Simone even wrote and recorded her own answer song. Lennon liked it, yet, with Yoko by his side, he strengthened his beliefs in pacifism.

The Beatles made promotional videos for 'Hey Jude' and 'Revolution', directed once more by Michael Lindsay-Hogg and performed in front of an audience at Twickenham Studios. The first airing of the video was to be on *The David Frost Show*, and so Frost was invited down to film an introduction to make the performance seem live when broadcast. He joked that they were 'the best tea-room orchestra in the world'.

74

SONGBOOK

THE BEATLES (known as THE WHITE ALBUM)

*There are so many songs (over thirty) that it
takes an awful lot of digesting and listening to.*
– Melody Maker

*I think it's a fine little album and the fact that it's
got so much on it is one of the things that's cool about it.*
– Paul McCartney

TRACK LIST

Side 1:

Back In The USSR (Lennon-McCartney)
Dear Prudence (Lennon-McCartney)
Glass Onion (Lennon-McCartney)
Ob-La-Di, Ob-La-Da (Lennon-McCartney)
Wild Honey Pie (Lennon-McCartney)
The Continuing Story Of Bungalow Bill (Lennon-McCartney)
While My Guitar Gently Weeps (Harrison)
Happiness Is A Warm Gun (Lennon-McCartney)

Side 2:

Martha My Dear (Lennon-McCartney)

I'm So Tired (Lennon-McCartney)
Blackbird (Lennon-McCartney)
Piggies (Harrison)
Rocky Raccoon (Lennon-McCartney)
Don't Pass Me By (Starkey)
Why Don't We Do It In The Road? (Lennon-McCartney)
I Will (Lennon-McCartney)
Julia (Lennon-McCartney)

Side 3:
Birthday (Lennon-McCartney)
Yer Blues (Lennon-McCartney)
Mother Nature's Son (Lennon-McCartney)
Everybody's Got Something To Hide Except Me And My Monkey (Lennon-McCartney)
Sexy Sadie (Lennon-McCartney)
Helter Skelter (Lennon-McCartney)
Long, Long, Long (Harrison)

Side 4:
Revolution 1 (Lennon-McCartney)
Honey Pie (Lennon-McCartney)
Savoy Truffle (Harrison)
Cry Baby Cry (Lennon-McCartney)
Revolution 9 (Lennon-McCartney)
Good Night (Lennon-McCartney)

Released: 22 November 1968 (Apple)
Highest chart position: 1
Weeks in chart: 17 (8 at number 1)

Before heading into Abbey Road, The Beatles gathered at George's house in Esher, Surrey, to put down demos of the twenty-three songs they had written while in Rishikesh, most of which made their way on to the White Album. Exceptions were: 'Junk' (it appeared on Paul's first solo album, *McCartney*), 'Circles' (recorded for George's solo album, *Gone Troppo*), 'Sour Milk Sea' (given to Apple artist Jackie Lomax as his first single), 'Not Guilty' (recorded on George's solo album, *Dark Horse*), 'What's The New Mary Jane' (unreleased until the third *Beatles Anthology* album), 'Child Of Nature' (reworked with different lyrics to become 'Jealous Guy' on *Imagine*), 'Mean Mr Mustard' and 'Polythene Pam' (both appeared on the *Abbey Road* medley).

The musical mood of 1968 took a U-turn from the psychedelic extravaganza of the previous year with a return to blues, folk and country – the roots of rock 'n' roll – and The Beatles, in Rishikesh writing songs on their acoustic guitars, reflected this mood across much of the album. Despite the peaceful and largely drug-free spell in India, many of the songs that came out of this meditative period were dark, unsettling and nerve-jangling. This fractious, undisciplined mood permeated the recording of the album with Paul's perfectionism – particularly while recording 'Ob-La-Di Ob-La-Da' – grating on his band members' nerves. John's new, all-consuming love for Yoko meant she was now a constant presence in the studio, and both of them were experimenting with heroin. Both George Martin and George Harrison left to go on holiday, the latter after particularly wearing sessions recording 110 unsuitable takes for his song, 'Not Guilty'. It wasn't unusual to find different Beatles in different studios recording different songs, and engineer

Geoff Emerick, pulled in too many different directions, also walked out of the sessions. Then, during an especially bad-tempered session for 'Back In The USSR', the normally easy-going Ringo not only walked out, but said he was leaving the group altogether – only to be coaxed back ten days later with his drums covered in flowers and his bandmates declaring him the best rock drummer in the world.

FAB FACT

Not every session was marred with bad humour and negative energy. During the session for 'Birthday', the band took a break together to watch the first showing on television of the film *The Girl Can't Help It*. Hugely influential to them all as youngsters, the film – which they probably hadn't seen since its cinema release in 1956 – featured their rock 'n' roll heroes Little Richard, Eddie Cochran, Fats Domino and Gene Vincent: a reminder of why they all got into music in the first place.

FAB FACT

John, Paul, George Martin, engineer Ken Scott and tape operator John Smith spent a twenty-four-hour session on 16–17 October sequencing the album to give us the sprawling, yet unimprovable album that was originally, and fittingly, to be called *A Doll's House*. Unfortunately, during the album's recording, the progressive folk band Family issued an album called *Music In A Doll's House*. It was Pop artist Richard Hamilton who came up with the solution: call the album, simply, *The Beatles*. Still, his iconic cover meant that it is now universally known as the White Album.

75

THE FIFTH BEATLE

ERIC CLAPTON

'Oh no. I can't do that. Nobody ever plays on The Beatles' records.'
– Eric Clapton to George Harrison

It was two months into the recording sessions for the White Album that George began work with the others on his first track for the album, 'While My Guitar Gently Weeps'; after only a day's rehearsal, the momentum dissipated over a few weeks. Unhappy with how the track was progressing, George brought in a reluctant Eric Clapton to Abbey Road as the band resumed work on 'While My Guitar Gently Weeps'. Clapton's magnificent guitar playing provided the extra ingredient that perfected the song.

Eric Patrick Clapton was born in Ripley, Surrey, on 30 March 1945. He grew up believing his grandmother, Rose, was his mother, and his real mother, Patricia Molly Clapton, was his big sister. The truth was that sixteen-year-old Patricia gave birth to Eric after an affair with a Canadian soldier, Edward Walter Fryer. He never met his real father and grew up a lonely, introverted kid.

He was given a guitar on his thirteenth birthday, though didn't really pick it up until he was fifteen and becoming a fan of blues music. He attended Kingston College of Art until being kicked out after his passion for music overtook his attendance of classes. Spending his spare time busking and developing his skills as a guitar player, he began to attract attention. By 1963, he had joined the Yardbirds, playing with them until their 1965 breakthrough hit, 'For Your Love'. More interested in the blues than pop success, he joined John Mayall and the Bluesbreakers, gaining a reputation for his guitar playing that, famously, saw one fan daub 'Clapton is God' on a wall in London. Then, in 1967, under the influence of Jimi Hendrix, who would become a close friend, he formed psychedelic-rock-jazz-blues supergroup Cream with drummer Ginger Baker and bassist Jack Bruce. Now he started to write songs and sing as well as play guitar, and had hits on both sides of the Atlantic. Despite their success, the band's interpersonal relationships were marred by creative tensions as well as drug and alcohol abuse, and Clapton followed up his stint with Cream starting other short-lived bands, Blind Faith and Derek and the Dominoes. Again, both these bands had successes but were stymied by excess.

Clapton was already within The Beatles' orbit by the time he played on 'While My Guitar Gently Weeps'. Earlier on in 1968, he guested on George Harrison's debut solo album *Wonderwall Music*, and they collaborated on Cream's last UK single, 'Badge'. Clapton also asked George to accompany him on tour with folk-blues band Bonnie and Delaney in the winter of 1969 while George was questioning his time within the Beatles machine. In December 1968, after the White Album's release, Clapton played guitar with John Lennon's Dirty Mac band (also starring Yoko Ono, Keith Richards and Mitch Mitchell from The Jimi Hendrix Experience) in the Rolling Stones' concert film *The Rolling Stones' Rock And Roll Circus*, playing 'Yer Blues' and jamming with violinist Ivry Gitlis on 'Whole Lotta Yoko'. Clapton joined John and Yoko again as part of the Plastic Ono Band on their single

George and Eric Clapton get off an aircraft in Denmark
during a Bonnie and Delaney tour, 1969. *Getty Images*

'Cold Turkey' and at performances in Toronto and London for
UNICEF.

His closeness with George resulted in an infatuation with Pattie
Harrison, and as he became more desperate by her unrequited
feelings and his own heroin addiction (at one point he had a
$16,000-weekly habit), Clapton wrote one of his best-known and
best-loved songs, 'Layla'.

By 1974, Clapton had kicked heroin and was now in a
relationship with Pattie. They married in 1979, with George,

Paul and Ringo in attendance, but divorced in 1989 when he embarked on a solo career that saw him become one of the country's most successful musicians. With a more FM-friendly rock sound, he went on to have many hits, including 'I Shot The Sheriff', 'Wonderful Tonight' and 'Tears In Heaven', and enjoyed collaborations with many musicians such as J.J. Cale, Bob Dylan, Phil Collins, Roger Waters and his hero, BB King. Clapton retired in 2014 after being diagnosed with peripheral neuropathy, though he still performs on special occasions and continues to record. He is now clean from drugs and alcohol and, in 1998, established the Crossroads Centre in Antigua to help others overcome their addiction issues.

After George Harrison's death in 2001, Clapton was the musical director of *Concert for George*, a show in the Royal Albert Hall dedicated to celebrating George's musical legacy.

In 2012, to celebrate his eightieth birthday, artist Peter Blake recreated the *Sgt. Pepper* album cover with the British cultural figures he most admires. Eric Clapton stands right at the front beside David Hockney, Ian Dury and Blake's daughter Daisy.

76

A DAY OF RECKONING:
THE MANSON MURDERS

It's The Beatles, the music they're putting out . . .
I hear what it relates. It says, 'Rise.' It says, 'Kill.'
Why blame it on me? I didn't write the music.
  – Charles Manson, during his trial

John liked to play games with his lyrics, to tease the 'pseuds' who sought hidden meaning in his writing. The White Album's 'Glass Onion' was Lennon's most pointed allusion to this, a song packed with self-references that mock The Beatles' own mythology. Regrettably, it was not only pseuds who could misinterpret his and his bandmates' work but damaged individuals, and, in 1969, the White Album found itself at the centre of one of America's most harrowing murder cases.

Charles Manson had a troubled childhood. He was born in 1934 to an alcoholic mother and absent father, and was in and out of juvenile and adult correctional facilities for much of his early life. By 1967, a pimp and a petty thief, he found himself in San Francisco's Haight-Ashbury district, the epicentre of hippie dropout culture. His charisma attracted a gang of followers – mostly young, vulnerable women he called the 'Manson Family' – which then developed into a Doomsday cult. In 1968, they travelled to LA and took residence in a dilapidated ranch just outside the city.

Manson was convinced he was a talented singer-songwriter and started to make contacts in the music industry. Through Beach Boy Dennis Wilson, he met Byrds producer and son of Doris Day, Terry Melcher, who invited him to his studio to lay down demos. They also discussed making a documentary about the Family, but Melcher was unsettled by Manson's behaviour and didn't think much of his songs. Manson was furious.

When the White Album came out, Manson was convinced that The Beatles were speaking directly to him. He conflated his obsession with the Book of Revelations with 'Helter Skelter', believing it to be a warning that an apocalyptic race war was just around the corner, a conflict that would see his Family take their place as rightful leaders. He interpreted 'Blackbird' and 'Rocky Raccoon' as further hints of Black Power, and 'Piggies' as confirmation of that the Establishment was due a day of reckoning.

When the deluded Manson felt that the race war was not coming quickly enough, he decided that the Family should speed things up. His solution was to kill affluent white people in an attempt to make the deaths appear racially motivated.

On 8 August 1969, Manson instructed members of the Family to go to Terry Melcher's house and kill everyone as gruesomely as possible. The property was occupied by Sharon Tate and Roman Polanski. Polanski was in London working on his latest film, and Tate, eight months' pregnant, was socialising with friends Jay Sebring, Wojciech Frykowski and Abigail Folger. They were all brutally murdered, and their blood was smeared on the walls with the slogan 'PIG'. Steven Parent, who was visiting the house's caretaker at the same time, was also killed. The next day, Manson, who was angry about the sloppiness of the murders the night before, took the Family to shop owners'

Leno and Rosemary LaBianca's house, where he tied them up and ordered their killing. Again, after their brutal stabbings, the Family daubed the house with bloody messages: 'Rise', 'Death to Pigs' and 'Healter [sic] Skelter'.

Manson and his cohorts were convicted of eight murders in total. Manson died behind bars, aged eighty-three, in 2017. Four months later, his ashes were scattered on a California hillside. The mourners included long-time Family member Sandy Good.

77

SONGBOOK

YELLOW SUBMARINE

You had this lovely, lovely land of brightness and colour. And everybody is smiling and happy and butterflies flitting around and it was that kind of image . . . it was like a dream world, really.
– George Martin

TRACK LIST

Side 1:
Yellow Submarine (Lennon-McCartney)
Only A Northern Song (Harrison)
All Together Now (Lennon-McCartney)
Hey Bulldog (Lennon-McCartney)
It's All Too Much (Harrison)
All You Need Is Love (Lennon-McCartney)

Side 2:
Pepperland
Sea Of Time
Sea Of Holes
Sea Of Monsters
March Of The Meanies
Pepperland Laid Waste

Yellow Submarine In Pepperland
(All of these compositions were written by George Martin as part of
the score for *Yellow Submarine*.)

Released: 17 January 1969 (Apple)
Highest chart position: 3
Weeks in chart: 10

FAB FACT

The majority of the songs that would end up on the *Yellow
Submarine* soundtrack were recorded during the sessions for *Sgt.
Pepper's Lonely Hearts Club Band* and *Magical Mystery Tour*. By the
time the film was in production and released, The Beatles were
concentrating on making the White Album.

FAB FACT

George has two songs on the soundtrack album, an indication
of John and Paul's disinterest in the project. 'It's All Too Much'
was written after an acid trip and features, in the fadeout, George
singing the opening lines of The Merseybeats' classic cover of
'Sorrow' as well as the trumpets riffing on Jeremiah Clarke's 'Prince
Of Denmark March'. His 'Only A Northern Song' was written as a
pointed joke towards Northern Songs, the company set up by Dick
James at the beginning of The Beatles' career to look after their
publishing rights.

FAB FACT

Although the film premiered in July 1968, the Martin songs that
made up the score were re-recorded for the soundtrack album with
a forty-one-piece orchestra conducted by Martin in sessions on
22 and 23 October. His score was evocative, and playful too, with

experimental techniques – music played backwards, sound effects and so on – he had learned from working with The Beatles. And there was a nod to the iconic Hamlet cigar commercials in the 'Sea Of Monsters' scene, with Bach's 'Air On The G String'.

78

GET BACK

*Got up went to Twickenham rehearsed
until lunch time left the Beatles*
– George Harrison diary entry, 10 January 1969

Following the unease of the White Album sessions, amid the increasing chaos of Apple Corps, and to move on from the ridicule meted out to John and Yoko following the release of their *Two Virgins* album, Paul suggested to the rest of The Beatles that they hit the road again to play shows in theatres across the UK.

The rest of the band were not keen: John and George's enthusiasm for being Beatles was dwindling by the day, and Ringo was about to start filming his second solo film project, *The Magic Christian*, in February. A single gig was proposed, at the Roundhouse in London, one that would be filmed for a television special by Michael Lindsay-Hogg. Head of Apple Film Denis O'Dell suggested filming the rehearsal footage too. Then Lindsay-Hogg, fresh off filming *The Rolling Stones' Rock and Roll Circus*, decided that the Roundhouse was too dull for a Beatles finale. An ocean liner was proposed, as were the Sahara desert, the Pyramids of Giza and a Roman amphitheatre in North Africa where an audience of people of different cultures, colours and creeds would fill the space as the sun rose.

The Beatles duly trooped into Twickenham Studios on 2 January to start rehearsing the tracks that were to make the new album, provisionally titled 'Get Back'. The atmosphere was negative from the get-go. Keeping to film-making hours rather than their usual recording hours, realising how rusty they were at playing together, and the unresolved tensions from the White Album sessions meant Twickenham was a cold, uninspiring and tetchy episode. Matters came to a head when George walked out after a blow-up with John, leaving The Beatles with the words, 'I'll see you in the clubs.'

He was coaxed back a week later after it was agreed that that they would no longer work at Twickenham, that the show in North Africa would be abandoned, and that they could concentrate on making their new album. The Beatles moved into the new studios in the basement of the Apple offices. Expecting the seventy-two-track studio promised by Magic Alex, they were sorely disappointed to discover nothing of the sort, only some speakers and a lot of mess. Martin had to borrow some recording equipment from EMI.

The band were keen that the new album would be back to basics: no editing, no overdubs, just raw, live Beatles magic. But they were no longer the tight, energetic rock 'n' roll band that could record an album in eleven hours flat, as they had in 1963, and recording take after take after take tried the patience of everyone, including Martin, who left the job of recording to engineer Glyn Johns.

The atmosphere improved when an old friend from their Hamburg days, Billy Preston – on tour with Ray Charles – rocked up to Apple on George's suggestion. Not only did he bring his brilliant keyboard skills, his good humour and warmth improved the mood of the sessions; with his help, The Beatles recorded their new songs and enjoyed jamming old rock 'n' roll and R&B favourites together.

79

👥👥

THE FIFTH BEATLE

BILLY PRESTON

*He was a warm, wonderful human being with a
mile-wide smile. He was also a genius musician,
the likes of whom we will not see again.*
– Roger Friedman

William Everett Preston was born on 2 September 1946 in Houston, Texas, and later moved to Los Angeles with his mother. He was a self-taught musician, and recognised as something of a child prodigy. By the age of ten, he was playing organ behind noted gospel singers, including Mahalia Jackson. He also starred as a young Nat King Cole in the Cole biopic *St. Louis Blues*.

By 1962, he was playing keyboard as part of Little Richard's backing band and he met The Beatles in Hamburg when they were Little Richard's support act in the Star Club. In 1963, he played on Sam Cooke's bluesy album *Night Beat*, and released his own instrumental album, *The Most Exciting Organ Ever*, in 1965.

By 1967, he was in demand as a session musician, and joined Ray Charles' band, touring with him across the world. In January 1969, after walking out of the 'Get Back' sessions, George caught the London show and invited him to come along to the studio once the band had relocated to Apple's basement. Preston played with them for nine days, from 22 to 31 January, and contributed to the

Let It Be album, as well as 'I Want You (She's So Heavy)', which appeared on *Abbey Road*. He was credited on their next single 'Get Back/Don't Let Me Down', and was with the band at their last-ever live performance on the rooftop of the Apple building.

After recording with the band, Preston signed to Apple and released an album, *That's The Way God Planned It*, in 1969. He stayed in touch with all four Beatles, appearing at George's Concert for Bangladesh and on several of his solo albums. He also worked with John and Ringo, and recorded with the Rolling Stones throughout the seventies. He had a string of his own hit singles and albums throughout the decade, winning a Grammy for Best Pop Instrumental Performance for 'Outa-Space'. In the eighties, his career stalled as he battled addictions, but he continued with his session work, recording with Luther Vandross and Whitney Houston, and touring with friends. After years of poor health, he died in 2006 in Arizona.

Billy Preston in 1969. *Getty Images*

80

UP ON THE ROOF

George didn't want to do it, and Ringo started saying he didn't really see the point. Then John said, 'Oh, fuck it – let's do it.'
– Michael Lindsay-Hogg

While The Beatles were in Apple rehearsing and recording their new songs, Michael Lindsay-Hogg was aware that the 'Get Back' film still needed a decent finale. It's contested who came up with the idea to perform on the roof of the Apple building – contenders are Paul, Ringo, Glyn Johns and even John, who was also heard at the time suggesting a gig in an asylum – but on Thursday, 30 January, on a cold, windy, foggy London day, and in front of around thirty friends, family and Apple employees, The Beatles gave their final public performance.

It was hoped that they would be arrested as a public nuisance, giving the end of the film extra spice, and a secret camera was installed at the entrance of the Apple building to catch the police coming into the building to put the band in cuffs. In the end, only one young constable, Ken Wharfe, who later went on to become Princess Diana's protection officer, arrived, wagging a finger, and with no drama ended their performance. John remarked, 'I'd like to say thanks on behalf of the group and ourselves, and I hope we passed the audition.'

They certainly had. Despite the lacklustre energy, bum notes, bitching and bad timing that had characterised the rehearsal sessions, when they plugged in on the roof they were as brilliant, funny and charming as they'd ever been. Paul strapped on his Hofner bass, which still had the setlist for the 1966 Candlestick Park show taped to it, and gave funky, full-throated performances of 'Get Back' and 'I've Got A Feeling', and John, obviously enjoying himself, was in fine voice for 'Dig A Pony' and 'Don't Let Me Down'. Both of them shared the vocal duties on 'One After 909', their harmonies tight and melodic, and happy glances were exchanged. George, Ringo and Billy Preston provided solid backing, in a day that would go down in history.

On the streets below, the public mood went from confused to delighted – though, of course, there were some grumpy naysayers, particularly the bowler-hatted accountants from the local offices who phoned the police. But for those who couldn't believe their luck in being so close to the Apple building, there were mad scrambles to their own roofs and windows to get as good a view as possible of The Beatles giving them all a sneaky preview of their new songs.

81

♦♦♦♦

SONGBOOK

GET BACK/DON'T LET ME DOWN

A-side:
Get Back (Lennon-McCartney)

B-side:
Don't Let Me Down (Lennon-McCartney)

Released: 11 April 1969 (Apple)
Highest chart position: 1
Weeks in chart: 13 (2 at number 1)

FAB FACT

Paul started writing 'Get Back' after reading a story about Kenyan Asians having trouble getting to Britain before the Commonwealth immigration bill that would deny them entry into the country was passed in the House of Commons. Originally a satire on those who espoused an anti-immigration stance – Enoch Powell's 'rivers of blood' speech was only months away – Paul changed his mind about the lyrics, mindful of how easy it would be to misinterpret his intent.

FAB FACT

'Get Back/Don't Let Me Down' was the only single that credited another musician. It was released with the credit 'The Beatles with Billy Preston'.

FAB FACT

In America, as the single reached the top spot, The Beatles surpassed Elvis Presley's record for the most number one hits in the *Billboard* chart.

82

BEATLE BUSTS

I find caffeine easier to deal with.
– John Lennon

On 12 March 1969, Paul married photographer Linda Eastman at Marylebone Register Office, to the sound of sobbing fans consoling each other outside. At the same time, George was working on Jackie Lomax's album at the Apple offices – he was due to attend Paul's reception at The Ritz later – when a call came through from Pattie: fifteen policemen and women, led by Detective Sergeant Norman Pilcher, had turned up at their door with sniffer dogs.

When George arrived home he found paparazzi in the bushes and the police brandishing a shoe with a large chunk of cannabis inside it. He admitted to having cannabis in the house but was sure there were underhand tactics at play. He commented at the time: 'I'm a tidy man. I keep my socks in the sock drawer and stash in the stash box. It's not mine.' Still, he and Pattie were found guilty of possession at the Esher & Walton Magistrates Court and were fined £250 each.

It wasn't the first time one of The Beatles had come up against the notorious Detective Sergeant Pilcher. He'd also busted Mick Jagger, Keith Richards, Brian Jones and Donovan. On 18 October 1968, he and a team of seven busted John and Yoko while they were staying at Ringo's London flat in Montagu Square. Fortunately, the pair, who had been using heroin, had received a tip-off from

John and Yoko leave Marylebone Magistrates Court, surrounded by
police, after being remanded on bail for possession of cannabis. *Alamy*

a friendly Fleet Street insider three weeks previously, and had cleaned up the flat. It's said that John personally vacuumed the flat to remove all traces, and Pete Shotton disposed of the hoover bag. When Pilcher and his team arrived, they could only find small amounts of cannabis in various locations, adding up to a measly half-ounce. At Marylebone Court, John took full responsibility for possession and was fined £150.

In November 1972, before a case against him came to court, Pilcher resigned from the police force. The following year, he was sentenced to four years' imprisonment for conspiracy to pervert the course of justice, though it was never proven that he did plant drugs in his celebrity busts. Given the tiny quantities, it seems unlikely.

Paul would come up against the law on several occasions during the seventies and eighties for marijuana possession, his most notorious bust while he was on tour with Wings in 1980. Arriving in Tokyo airport, customs discovered half a pound of marijuana in his luggage and accused him of smuggling. He protested that it was only for personal use, but he spent nine days behind bars before the Japanese government released him without filing charges.

Ringo, despite his well-documented troubles with drink and drugs after The Beatles split, kicked his bad habits in rehab, and did not come up against the long arm of the law throughout his career.

83

SONGBOOK

THE BALLAD OF JOHN AND YOKO/
OLD BROWN SHOE

A-side:
The Ballad Of John And Yoko (Lennon-McCartney)

B-side:
Old Brown Shoe (Harrison)

Released: 30 May 1969 (Apple)
Highest chart position: 1
Weeks in chart: 14 (3 at number 1)

FAB FACT

As 'The Ballad Of John And Yoko' was an unscheduled release, their previous single 'Get Back' was still in the Top 10 when it reached the top spot.

FAB FACT

When John and Yoko got together, their lives became a perpetual art project. They collaborated on avant-garde albums and art shows, planted acorns for peace at Coventry Cathedral, gigged at Cambridge University where John accompanied Yoko's freestyle wailing, and introduced Bagism, their version of 'total communication' at the Albert Hall in 1968. Their wedding, honeymoon bed-in in Amsterdam and Bagism event in Vienna documented in 'The Ballad Of John And Yoko' was their most high-profile project yet. Keen to use their platform to promote peace to a wide audience, their efforts were frequently panned by either a patronising or a hostile press who didn't, or chose not to, understand that John and Yoko's actions were deliberately provocative, playful and absurd. As John said to journalists, 'We are happy to be the world's clowns.'

FAB FACT

With Ringo away filming *The Magic Christian* with Peter Sellers, and George abroad, only John and Paul feature in the song. Despite their behind-the-scenes troubles with Apple and future manager Allen Klein, the song was recorded with great energy and in good spirits.

FAB FACT

John and Yoko would go on to host another bed-in later in 1969 in Montreal, where John composed and recorded 'Give Peace A Chance' (released with Yoko as Plastic Ono Band). Present at the recording of the song were, amongst others, Allen Ginsberg, Timothy Leary, Murray the K, Dick Gregory and Petula Clark. The song was attributed to Lennon-McCartney as a thank you to Paul for helping out with the composing and recording of 'The Ballad Of John And Yoko', and peaked at number two in the UK chart.

Opposite: John and Yoko advertise peace outside the Apple offices in 1969. *Alamy*

84

APPLE GOES SOUR

We had every freak in the world coming in there.
– George Harrison

Apple, The Beatles' version of 'western communism', came up against problems almost as soon as it began. The first casualty of their venture was the boutique. Pete Shotton, who had some retail management experience, soon left, the more outlandish ideas and practices of design collective The Fool clashing with his more pragmatic approach. The shop went through a string of managers, at one point being run by a tarot card reader called Caleb. Shoplifting was constant. In seven months, the boutique lost around £200,000, and it was no hard decision to close it. They gave away all the stock (after The Beatles nabbed the best stuff for themselves).

As the offices moved from Baker Street to Wigmore Street to Savile Row, with each move came snazzy new interior design – plush green carpet, beautiful oak furniture, stunning objets d'art – as well as expense accounts at Fortnum & Mason and in-house cordon bleu chefs. Apple became the hottest hangout in town. San Franciscan Hells Angels Frisco Pete and Billy Tumbleweed came over with an army of hangers-on, charging The Beatles with the shipping costs for their bikes, and terrifying the children at the 1968 office Christmas party. A family of American hippies moved in and attempted to persuade John to bankroll their dream of an island commune in Fiji but were placated with a home on Lennon's island, Dorinish, off the coast of County Mayo in Ireland. Theft was rife: TVs, typewriters, cases of wine all vanished under the arms of cheeky opportunists – even the lead from the roof. And though Apple Music was bringing in money with successes from The Beatles, Mary Hopkin, Badfinger and the Radha Krishna Temple, there were, unfortunately, far too many releases – Jackie Lomax, Black Dyke Mills Brass Band, Doris Troy, White Trash – that didn't chart, despite a lot of love and attention from Derek Taylor's adventurous press team.

The Beatles' accountants fired off memos warning of overspending, but they fell on deaf ears. At last, it was agreed that Apple would bring in someone to take control of the finances. Lord Beeching, who had just gutted the UK's railway network, was approached, but he declined; Lord Poole, the Queen's financial adviser, and Lord Arnold Goodman, Prime Minister Harold Wilson's economic adviser, were also suggested.

In early 1969, John gave a loose-lipped interview to journalist Ray Coleman in which he asserted that The Beatles would be 'broke in six months' if Apple didn't straighten itself out, much to the interest of one man at his desk in New York City . . .

Crowds gather round the Apple Boutique as the stock is given away before its closure.
Getty Images

85

THE FIFTH BEATLE

ALLEN KLEIN

Though I walk in the valley of the shadow of evil,
I have no fear, as I am the biggest bastard in the valley.
– Allen Klein's desk display

Allen Klein was born in New Jersey on 18 December 1931, the fourth child of Hungarian Jewish immigrants. When he was very young, his mother died, and he and his sisters were placed in an orphanage until his father remarried when Klein was ten years old.

After he graduated from high school he found work with a magazine and newspaper distributor and enlisted in the army, serving as a clerk in New York. After his service he studied accountancy at Upsala College, and found a job with a Manhattan accountancy firm charged with auditing music publishers and agencies. His unique skill was his ability to find money owed to artists; he famously made Bobby Darin his first million and renegotiated Sam Cooke's contract with RCA. He worked with The Animals, Herman's Hermits, Donovan and The Dave Clark Five, then renegotiated The Rolling Stones' deal with Decca, which ensured that they, despite selling fewer records, made more money than The Beatles.

Klein had always wanted to manage pop's biggest prize asset, and he'd approached (and was rebuffed by) Epstein in 1964. After reading John's comments to Ray Coleman, Klein phoned Apple to ask to speak to The Beatles. In a placatory move after endless phone calls, Derek Taylor suggested he meet John and Yoko in The Dorchester. Klein bowled them both over with his knowledge of John's songs and Yoko's art, and with his street-smart attitude, something that impressed George and Ringo too when John introduced Klein to the rest of the band. Paul was not quite so captivated; he was keen that his new in-laws would look after The Beatles' financial interests, and even tried to bring in Mick Jagger to persuade them that Klein's business dealings were not always above board. Jagger was not an effective voice of dissent, and John, George and Ringo, suspicious that keeping it in the Eastman family would mean favourable treatment to Paul, were still convinced that Klein should manage the group. While unable to resolve this uneasy stand-off, Klein was tasked to examine the finances of Apple and The Beatles' contracts with EMI and Capitol, United Artists, Northern Songs and NEMS, while the Eastmans were allowed to offer legal advice on the future of Apple. It was an uneasy compromise, their cooperation marred by paranoia and secret scheming.

At Apple, amongst many belt-tightening measures, there were multiple firings. Out went Ron Kass, Alistair 'Mr Fixit' Taylor, Brian Lewis, Magic Alex and a swathe of secretaries and PAs as well as the in-house translator and kitchen staff. Peter Asher left in protest, taking James Taylor with him. Apple also ended its schools programme, the film and electronic divisions, and, despite having work deep in production on spoken word label Zapple (including recordings from Ken Kesey, Charles Bukowski, Ken Weaver of The Fugs, Lawrence Ferlinghetti, Richard Brautigan and other countercultural luminaries) it was also shut down. Many of the Zapple recordings were released by other labels.

Allen Klein with John and Yoko in the Apple offices. *Getty Images*

Then, NEMS sold seventy per cent of their shares to Triumph Investment Trust resulting in EMI freezing The Beatles' royalties until Klein, who had boasted to the band that he could get them NEMS for nothing, negotiated a deal with Triumph that cost the band more than the £1 million offer the Eastmans had originally suggested.

While dealing with NEMS and Triumph, Dick James, who had started Northern Songs to look after the Lennon-McCartney publishing rights back in 1963, sold his shares to ATV. Now, both The Beatles and ATV owned thirty-five per cent each of the company, and it was up to Klein to make sure The Beatles became the majority shareholders by negotiating with the consortium that owned the remaining shares. He failed. The consortium sold to ATV, and by the end of 1969 ATV owned ninety-two per cent of the company.

However, Klein did manage to salvage his reputation when he renegotiated The Beatles' contract with EMI and Capitol in a history-making deal, one that even Paul admitted he could find no fault in. Paul finally succumbed, and agreed, with some caveats, on a management contract with Klein.

Klein continued to manage The Beatles after their official split in 1970, and assisted John and Yoko with the *Imagine* film, and George with the Concert for Bangladesh. However, his relationship with John, George and Ringo soured due to the financial arrangements he made for the concert and film, and they fired him as their manager. He sued them for $19 million, but settled for $4.2 million in 1977. That same year he was charged with income tax evasion – though only one charge stuck in the end – and he spent two months in jail in 1980. He later managed Phil Spector's business affairs, and forced The Verve to sell the rights to their hit single 'Bittersweet Symphony' to him for $1 due to their sample of the strings of the Andrew Loog Oldham Orchestra's version of 'The Last Time' owned by his company ABKCO. He died of Alzheimer's disease in New York in 2009.

86

SONGBOOK

ABBEY ROAD

Everybody worked frightfully well, and that's why I'm very fond of it.
– George Martin

Now we can just sit back, relax and enjoy Beatle offerings
and appreciate them on their own level. Too much has passed
under the bridge to start getting uptight, and the truth is,
their latest LP is just a natural born gas, entirely free
of pretension, deep meanings or symbolism.
– Melody Maker

TRACK LIST

Side 1:
Come Together (Lennon-McCartney)
Something (Harrison)
Maxwell's Silver Hammer (Lennon-McCartney)
Oh! Darling (Lennon-McCartney)
Octopus's Garden (Starkey)
I Want You (*She's So Heavy*) (Lennon-McCartney)

Side 2:
Here Comes The Sun (Harrison)

Because (Lennon-McCartney)
You Never Give Me Your Money (Lennon-McCartney)
Sun King (Lennon-McCartney)
Mean Mr Mustard (Lennon-McCartney)
Polythene Pam (Lennon-McCartney)
She Came In Through The Bathroom Window (Lennon-McCartney)
Golden Slumbers (Lennon-McCartney)
Carry That Weight (Lennon-McCartney)
The End (Lennon-McCartney)
Her Majesty (Lennon-McCartney)

Released: 26 September 1969 (Apple)
Highest chart position: 1
Weeks in chart: 97 (17 at number 1)

FAB FACT

With the *Get Back/Let it Be* sessions languishing, unloved by the band, in the hands of engineer Glyn Johns, Paul, after speaking with the others, phoned Martin to ask him if he wanted to make an album with the band 'like they used to'. Although they didn't know for certain that *Abbey Road* would be the last album they recorded together, there was a sense of galvanising each other after the disinterest in Twickenham and Apple.

FAB FACT

George was the first musician in Britain to own a Moog synthesiser, which he brought to the *Abbey Road* sessions. The instrument features on four tracks: 'Because', 'Here Comes The Sun', 'Maxwell's Silver Hammer' and 'I Want You (She's So Heavy)'.

John missed the first sessions for the album as he and Yoko were recovering in hospital in the Scottish Highlands after a crash in their Austin Maxi. They'd been travelling to Durness in Sutherland for a holiday with their children, Julian and Kyoko. John had hardly been behind the wheel since passing his test in 1965 and was known to be a hopeless driver. He remarked at the time that 'if you're going to have a car crash, try to arrange for it to happen in the Highlands. The hospital there was just great.'

Abbey Road features 'Octopus's Garden', the second Beatles song written by Ringo, which he wrote after a conversation with a fisherman in Sardinia when he left the band during the White Album sessions.

John wrote 'Because' after hearing Yoko playing Beethoven's *Moonlight Sonata*. When it came to performing the close harmonies in the studio, The Beatles set the mood by dimming the lights and lighting incense. John, Paul and George sat close together in a semi-circle with Ringo guiding them to time through their headphones. They sang together in one track, which was then overdubbed to make a nine-part harmony. It was the last time all four of them recorded in the studio together.

John's 'Mean Mr Mustard' was inspired by a story he read in the *Daily Record* newspaper of 7 June 1967 about a Scottish civil servant, John Mustard, whose meanness made his wife Freda's life unendurable. When she divorced him, she described how her husband would shave in the dark to save light and how in the last year before they separated he gave her £1. The judge decided that Mr Mustard had gone 'far beyond what any wife could be expected to bear' and granted her a divorce.

FAB FACT

The hidden track 'Her Majesty' is the shortest song recorded by The Beatles, all 23 seconds of it.

87

SONGBOOK

SOMETHING/COME TOGETHER

A-side:
Something (Harrison)

A-side:
Come Together (Lennon-McCartney)

Released: 8 November 1969 (Apple)
Highest chart position: 4
Weeks in chart: 12

FAB FACT

It was Allen Klein's idea to release 'Something/Come Together'
as a single, the first time a Beatles song had been released *after* its
inclusion on an album.

FAB FACT

'Something' was written during the White Album sessions, but not
fully worked on until mid-1969. Over the sessions, George was
unsure about his guitar solo and had to record with the orchestra
as there were no room for more overdubs. His performance when
it came to recording was note-perfect and emotionally resonant.

FAB FACT

'Something' is the second-most covered Beatles' song after 'Yesterday'. It's been recorded by hundreds of artists, and was memorably described by Frank Sinatra as 'the greatest love song of the past fifty years'.

FAB FACT

When John met Timothy Leary in Canada, Leary was campaigning to become Governor of California, running against Ronald Reagan. His campaign slogan was 'Come Together, Join the Party', and he asked John to write him a campaign song. Instead, John took the phrase and composed this rumbling, bluesy countercultural shout-out.

FAB FACT

With its opening line echoing the Chuck Berry song 'You Can't Catch Me', John was sued by Morris Levy, the copyright owners of Berry's music. As part of the court settlement, John agreed to record 'You Can't Catch Me' and other Levy-owned rock 'n' roll numbers, Berry's 'Sweet Little Sixteen' and Lee Dorsey's 'Ya Ya', which formed part of his *Rock 'n' Roll* album released in 1975.

88

PAUL IS DEAD

I am alive and well and unconcerned about the rumours of
my death. But if I were dead, I would be the last to know.
– Paul McCartney

There were always strange rumours circulating about The Beatles
in the press, and normally they didn't cause too much of a fuss.
But in the latter half of 1969, one such rumour caused many
Beatles fans to lose their minds.

On 17 September, an article was published in the *Northern Star*,
the newspaper for the Northern Illinois University. It declared that
Paul McCartney was dead, and had been dead since a car crash
in 1966, whereupon it had been decided to replace him with a
lookalike and soundalike, William Shears Campbell (shortened to
Billy Shears, who was introduced to us on the *Sgt. Pepper* album),
so that The Beatles could carry on and the fans didn't have to grieve.
Not only that, but The Beatles had been laying out clues to this
truth in their singles and albums since his death.

The rumour spread to the Detroit radio station WKNR when
a DJ held a phone-in to lay out the evidence. Their new album,
Abbey Road, was a key text in the conspiracy, offering the following
clues:

• The band were walking across the road as if in a funeral procession:
John as the clergyman, Ringo as the undertaker, Paul as the corpse

(he was barefoot after all) and George as the gravedigger.

• Paul, who was known to be left-handed, held his cigarette in his right hand. Imposter!

• The Volkswagen Beetle car had a number plate that ended 28IF, the age he would be *if* he was still alive. (He was actually twenty-seven on the release of *Abbey Road*.)

And the fans didn't stop at *Abbey Road* searching for clues. Other 'evidence' mounted:

• If you play 'Revolution 9' backwards, you can hear the words 'turn me on, dead man'.

• On the White Album, in between 'Blackbird' and 'I'm So Tired', John mumbles, 'Paul is dead, man, miss him, miss him.'

• If you listen closely to the fadeout of 'Strawberry Fields Forever', you can hear John intoning 'I buried Paul'. (He actually says 'cranberry sauce'.)

• If you look at the picture of The Beatles on the back of the *Sgt. Pepper* album, Paul is the only band member turning his back on us, the audience.

• In the centrefold picture in the *Sgt. Pepper* album, Paul is wearing a black armband with the initials 'OPD', the acronym Canada uses for 'Officially Pronounced Dead'.

• During the 'Your Mother Should Know' scene in *Magical Mystery Tour*, Paul is wearing a black rose while the others wear red ones.

Sales of Beatles albums soared in the US, and both *Sgt. Pepper* and *Magical Mystery Tour* re-entered the US *Billboard* charts as fans pored over them trying to find clues.

Of course, Paul was not dead; he had only retreated to his farm in Scotland with Linda and the kids and Martha the Old English

Sheepdog to take a break from his Beatle stresses. *Life* magazine finally tracked him down to his home on the Mull of Kintyre, though Paul's first reaction to their intrusion was to throw a bucket of water over the journalist and photographer. Realising that the angry images would damage his reputation, he agreed to speak to them in return for the photographs that had been taken. The McCartney family returned to London in December 1969, still alive and well.

89

SONGBOOK

LET IT BE/
YOU KNOW MY NAME
(LOOK UP THE NUMBER)

A-side:
Let It Be (Lennon-McCartney)

B-side:
You Know My Name (Look Up The Number) (Lennon-McCartney)

Released: 6 March 1970 (Apple)
Highest chart position: 2
Weeks in chart: 17

FAB FACT

The inspiration for 'Let It Be' came from a dream. Paul, increasingly affected by the strains of his life as a Beatle, had a dream where his mother, Mary, told him that he would be okay and to let go of his stress.

FAB FACT

The single was released to try to temper the persistent media commentary that The Beatles were no more. At the time, their split was not public knowledge.

'You Know My Name (Look Up The Number)' is one of The Beatles' strangest releases. Recorded in 1967 and 1969, the song started off with John creating a mantra, and then moved on to include The Beatles jamming different musical styles – a ska section was edited out of the final version – along with comedic ad libbing. Paul invited Brian Jones to the studio to take part in the session, and the Rolling Stone turned up with a saxophone instead of an instrument he was actually skilled in playing. (And he was skilled in many.) Such was the good humour, though, that he joined in and did his best.

In November 1969, John tried to release 'You Know My Name (Look Up The Number)' as a single by the Plastic Ono Band with another comedic jam, 'What's The New Mary Jane', as its B-side. The plan was vetoed by his bandmates. 'What's The New Mary Jane' was later released as part of the *Anthology* project.

♦ ★ ★ ♦

90

THE FIFTH BEATLE

PHIL SPECTOR

I can't stand to be talked about. I can't stand to be looked at.
I can't stand to be photographed. I can't stand the attention.
But at the same time I want the recognition.
– Phil Spector to biographer Mick Brown

Harvey Phillip Spector was born on 26 December 1939, in the South Bronx, New York, to a first-generation immigrant Ukrainian family. Spector claimed that his parents, Benjamin and Bertha, were first cousins. They both loved music, and the radio was always on in the family home. After Benjamin committed suicide when Spector was nine years old, Bertha moved the family to Los Angeles where she worked as a seamstress.

Spector was an introverted boy and physically frail; he suffered from asthma and borderline diabetes, and detested the outdoors Californian lifestyle of beach, sun and sports. But he had a passion for music, and Bertha bought him a guitar for his thirteenth birthday. At high school he started a group, The Teddy Bears, with his friends. He was also taught studio production by Stan Ross, record producer and co-owner of Gold Star Studios in Hollywood, and, in 1958, the Teddy Bears hit the top of the *Billboard* Hot 100 chart (and number two in the UK) with a ballad penned by Spector, 'To Know Him Is To Love Him'. The

A nervous flyer, Phil Spector, on the same flight as The Beatles as they travel to New York for the first time. *Alamy*

title was borrowed from the epitaph on his father's gravestone. The song was their only hit, but through this first foray into recording he was invited to New York to work as an apprentice to the Leiber and Stoller songwriting and production team.

By the early sixties, he had started his own record company, Philles Records, and had discovered and produced successful acts such as The Crystals – scoring a number one hit, 'He's A Rebel', with them in 1963 – Bob B. Soxx & the Blue Jeans, Darlene Love and The Ronettes, who just missed the top spot with 'Be My Baby'. By Christmas 1963 and the release of his now classic Christmas album, Phil Spector's ingenious layered Wall of Sound production style had become more famous than the acts themselves.

He went on to produce smash hits for The Righteous Brothers, but was deeply affected by the US chart failure of his work with

Ike and Tina Turner on the magisterial 'River Deep, Mountain High' (the song reached number three in the UK chart).

In London, Allen Klein introduced Spector to John Lennon, and within days he was producing 'Instant Karma!', Lennon's solo single. Released in February 1970, it peaked in the UK chart at number five, and hit number three in the States. After that success John, George and Klein agreed to appoint Spector to salvage the *Get Back* tapes. He went through numerous outtakes and overhauled the lot, adding his signature strings and a brass section (and notably, a celestial harp and choir on 'The Long And Winding Road', which enraged Paul). 'Winding Road' would be the last of The Beatles' singles to be released in America (it remained an album track in the UK). Despite receiving some harsh criticism from the press, it sold 1.2 million copies in two days and reached number one in the States. The album *Let It Be* won a Grammy, and Paul collected the award.

Spector went on to work with several musicians, including collaborations with Leonard Cohen and The Ramones, as well as on several solo ventures for both George and John. His production of *Imagine*, John's most commercially successful album, was arguably the finest accomplishment in his long and remarkable career.

Spector's volatile personality and his increasingly public gunplay came to affect both his personal and professional relationships and, after 1980, he started to lead a more reclusive life. In 2003, the actress Lana Clarkson was found dead from a single gunshot wound in Spector's California home. In 2009, he was found guilty of second-degree murder and sentenced to nineteen years. He is currently serving his sentence in the California Health Care Facility.

91

SONGBOOK

LET IT BE

Well, it was too good to be true – somebody apparently just couldn't Let It Be, with the result that they put the load on their new friend P. Spector, who in turn whipped out his orchestra and choir and proceeded to turn several of the rough gems on the best Beatle album in ages into costume jewelry.
– Rolling Stone

I like what Phil did, actually.
– Ringo Starr

TRACK LIST

Side 1:
Two Of Us (Lennon-McCartney)
Dig A Pony (Lennon-McCartney)
Across The Universe (Lennon-McCartney)
I Me Mine (Harrison)
Dig It (Lennon-McCartney-Harrison-Starkey)
Let It Be (Lennon-McCartney)
Maggie Mae (trad. arr. Lennon-McCartney-Harrison-Starkey)

Side 2:

I've Got A Feeling (Lennon-McCartney)
One After 909 (Lennon-McCartney)
The Long And Winding Road (Lennon-McCartney)
For You Blue (Harrison)
Get Back (Lennon-McCartney)

Released: 8 May 1970 (Apple)
Highest chart position: 1
Weeks in chart: 53 (3 at number 1)

FAB FACT

Glyn Johns was charged with putting together an album from the many hours of tape recorded during the sessions at Twickenham, Apple and on the roof. Aware of the initial motivation of the 'Get Back' project to show The Beatles raw and real and to document the making of the album, Johns included studio conversations, false starts and jammed cover versions to create a live, unpolished atmosphere. When he presented his finished work to The Beatles, they vetoed its release. Phil Spector was drafted in, in March 1970, to complete what Johns had started, though in a move away from the 'no overdub' rule, he introduced session musicians to create his signature orchestral and choral backdrops to some of the songs.

FAB FACT

Before the rejection of Glyn Johns' work, the photograph for the 'Get Back' album cover art was taken. In a nod to the release of their first album, *Please Please Me*, the same photographer, Angus McBean, was used, and they recreated the picture with John, Paul, George and Ringo leaning over the balcony of the EMI offices.

The picture wasn't used for *Let It Be*, but both McBean pictures were resurrected for the official 'best of' albums, *The Red Album* and *The Blue Album*.

FAB FACT

The last-ever Beatles session at Abbey Road was to tidy up George's 'I Me Mine' when they learned that it was featuring in Michael Lindsay-Hogg's film. John was abroad, but Paul, George and Ringo got together to finish it off and work on a couple of 'Let It Be' overdubs on 3 and 4 January 1970.

FAB FACT

The album was released after The Beatles' split was finally announced, and, in Britain, was released as a special box-set album complete with book of photographs and printed dialogue from conversations between The Beatles during the rehearsal and recording sessions. A more conventional edition of the album was released on 6 November 1970.

92

ON THE SILVER SCREEN

LET IT BE

This unusual colour documentary serves, too, to highlight the poor value of the soundtrack album just released . . . Where Let It Be *scores is in its music; in the sharp editing and approach of producer Neil Aspinall; in moments to be savoured like the pipe-smoking, trilby-hatted gent walking over rooftops to see the Beatles playing on the Apple roof, for all the world as if he did it every day; in its humour; and in what it tells us about four often unlikeable yet likeable people.*
– NME

It was hell making the film . . . When it came out a lot of people complained about Yoko looking miserable in it. But even the biggest Beatle fan couldn't have sat through those six weeks of misery.
– John Lennon

And so, on the rooftop, on a cold January day in 1969, Michael Lindsay-Hogg and his team packed up their cameras, the solution for their film's finale found.

The next day, in the studio, there was no sense of excitement or satisfaction of a job complete amongst the Fabs, only relief that the cameras were no longer present. This ambivalence to the project continued as the footage was now in the care of the film's editor, Tony Lenny.

In July 1969, The Beatles were shown a rough cut of the film, which ran to an epic 210 minutes. The band were unimpressed, with Paul, George and Ringo particularly objecting to the sheer volume of John and Yoko footage. Klein, with some uncharacteristic diplomacy, directed Lindsay-Hogg to make the film about The Beatles and their music rather than their personal relationships, thus solving the issue.

By October 1969, the film had been cut to 100 minutes and was screened again with Paul, George and Ringo in attendance. Minor cuts were suggested, but the film was approved.

In spring 1970, Klein suggested the film and album's title be changed to *Let It Be* and scheduled the release of the single of the same name, deeming 'Get Back' old hat a year on from its release. He made another suggestion, with income as a motivating factor, that the film should be given a cinematic release rather than a television broadcast, and the footage was transferred from 16mm to 35mm film, resulting in a grainier look that could be explained away as cinéma vérité authenticity.

By the time the film was released, The Beatles were no more, and it was neither a critical nor a commercial success: the critics were disappointed in such a low-key swansong, and the fans were just not ready to see their beloved group in such a raw, unvarnished and uncomfortable state. But the band's musical gifts, despite their disarray, were still adored and The Beatles won an Oscar and a Grammy for Best Original Song Score and Best Original Music Soundtrack.

The film has had sporadic releases for home entertainment, but has mainly been viewed after its cinema release through pirate copies. In 2020, a new version of the film was due to be released under the direction of Peter Jackson, using the same stunning colourisation techniques he used in his First World War documentary *They Shall Not Grow Old*. Unfortunately, due to the COVID-19 pandemic, its release has been postponed until 2021. As well as the cinema release, a remastered version of the original *Let It Be* will be released on DVD.

93

AND IN THE END

*I'd loved them since I'd first heard them as a college freshman,
pouring all my quarters into the jukebox to play 'I Want To
Hold Your Hand'. . . When it was over, it was sad, but it
was time. We were fortunate they made the sacrifice to
be together with each other for so long.*
– Booker T.

The Beatles had weathered both Ringo and George's walkouts,
but, by the late summer of 1969, it was John's turn to decide
The Beatles were over. On Saturday, 13 September, John, and
his hastily put together Plastic Ono Band – Yoko, Eric Clapton,
Klaus Voormann and Andy White – played a rock 'n' roll revival
gig in Toronto alongside acts such as Chuck Berry, Little Richard,
Bo Diddley, Alice Cooper and The Doors. Along for the ride
were Allen Klein and journalist Ray Connolly (later the author of
many Beatles memoirs). On the flight home, John announced his
intention to leave The Beatles. Klein, at that time still negotiating
on The Beatles' behalf, advised John to keep schtum about his
decision, and Connolly was sworn to secrecy.

John kept his promise until Klein presented the new EMI/
Capitol contract for a ceremonial signing photograph at the Apple
offices. Ink dry and flashbulb dimmed, John informed Paul and
Ringo (George was absent that day) that he wanted a 'divorce'.
Paul and Ringo were stunned, but again it was decided that the

news should remain private as *Abbey Road* was days from release.

By early 1970, each Beatle was concentrating on solo projects: John and Yoko carried on publicising issues important to them and recorded and released the 'Cold Turkey' and 'Instant Karma' singles; George had gone on tour with folk band Bonnie and Delaney and was contemplating his first commercial solo album; while both Paul and Ringo were nearing completion of their first solo albums, *McCartney* and *Sentimental Journey*.

The 'Get Back' album and film were now back on track, both renamed *Let It Be*. Paul, now absent from Apple since John's decision, was astonished to learn that Spector had been brought in to rework Glyn Johns' tapes, as was George Martin – neither had been consulted. When Paul heard Spector's treatment of 'The Long And Winding Road', he fired off an irate letter to Klein to make known his disapproval, to no avail.

The last Beatles photo shoot, in August 1969, in John and Yoko's newly purchased Tittenhurst Park estate. *Getty Images*

The final straw for Paul was a visit from Ringo, despatched by Klein, John and George, to let him know that, with the release of both *Let It Be* and his *Sentimental Journey*, it had been decided to postpone the release of *McCartney* (it had been pencilled in for an April release). Paul went ballistic, sending Ringo packing. In the end, Ringo brought forward *Sentimental Journey* for a late March release, Paul kept his April release date, and *Let It Be* was scheduled for release on 8 May.

Paul had stopped doing his usual press rounds since late 1969, and was in no mood to put on his showbiz face for his solo album. He knew he'd have to fend off questions about The Beatles' future. Instead, he instructed the Apple press office to send him a Q&A to complete, to be included in the advance press copies of *McCartney*. When the journalists opened up their press packs, The Beatles' situation was crystal clear:

Q: Did you miss the other Beatles and George Martin? Was there a moment, e.g., when you thought, 'Wish Ringo was here for this break'?

A: No.

Q: Assuming this is a very big hit album, will you do another?

A: Even if it isn't, I will continue to do what I want – when I want to.

Q: Are you planning a new album or single with The Beatles?

A: No.

Q: Is this album a rest away from The Beatles or the start of a solo career?

A: Time will tell. Being a solo album means it's 'the start of a solo career' . . . and not being done with The Beatles means it's a rest. So it's both.

Q: Have you any plans for live appearances?

A: No.

Q: Is your break with The Beatles temporary or permanent, due to personal differences or musical ones?

A: Personal differences, business differences, but most of all because I have a better time with my family. Temporary or permanent? I don't know.

Q: Do you foresee a time when Lennon-McCartney becomes an active songwriting partnership again?

A: No.

On 10 April 1970, Paul's comments became headline news. As the world reeled from the revelation, Derek Taylor released this press statement:

> *Spring is here and Leeds play Chelsea tomorrow and Ringo and John and George and Paul are alive and well and full of hope.*
>
> *The world is still spinning and so are we and so are you. When the spinning stops – that'll be the time to worry. Not before.*
>
> *Until then, The Beatles are alive and well and the Beat goes on, the Beat goes on.*

When the *Let It Be* album was released, The Beatles were over. At the premieres of the *Let It Be* film in New York, London and Liverpool, no Beatle was present. Activity in Apple dried up, and by the end of 1970, its only function was to collect Beatles royalties.

On 1 January 1971, Paul sued his bandmates to officially dissolve The Beatles partnership that bound their earnings together through Apple and to oversee the separation of their assets.

94

BEATLES v. STONES

I would like to just list what we did and what the Stones did two months after, on every fuckin' *album and every* fuckin' *thing we did, Mick does exactly the same. He imitates us.*
– John Lennon, *Rolling Stone*, 1970

Are you Beatles or are you Stones? Since 1963, the answer to that question is supposed to signify what kind of person you are. It was an effective marketing and publicity ploy at a time when the music industry was reinventing itself to reflect societal shifts, yet the projected narrative of The Beatles as cuddly mop tops versus the Stones as rebel roustabouts is now recognised as overly simplistic. Still, there's no doubt that both bands' career choices encouraged each other to both characterise and shift the cultural conversation. Let's look at how their friendship and rivalry played out . . .

Rivals – It's October 1962, and Brian Jones turns on the radio in the flat he shares with his bandmates Mick Jagger and Keith Richards. The Rollin' Stones have been enjoying making a name for themselves in blues clubs around London. 'Love Me Do' is playing, the first single from a new band from Liverpool called The Beatles. Brian's spirits drop, Keith swears out loud, Mick feels sick: the harmonica and bluesy style on the record punctures their sense of their own originality. They feel like they need to keep an eye on this group.

Friends – On 14 April 1963, club owner Giorgio Gomelsky invites The Beatles and their entourage to the Crawdaddy, to see a band who have been causing a stir with his customers: the Rollin' Stones. The Beatles come along and are impressed, and after the show join the band back at their flat to talk and play music and get to know each other. In The Beatles' entourage is their publicity assistant, Andrew Loog Oldham, who has an epiphany watching the Rollin' Stones perform. He is going to be their new manager. He asks Brian Epstein to go into partnership with him, but when Epstein declines, he partners up with Eric Easton, another experienced impresario, instead, and they sign up the fledgling band. Oldham's PR instincts tell him that the band should adapt their name to the Rolling Stones, that Keith Richards should drop the 's' from his surname and their ages need to be reduced by a few years. More showbiz appeal!

John Lennon and Mick Jagger while filming
The Rolling Stones Rock and Roll Circus. Alamy

Friends – George Harrison and Dick Rowe, the man who famously turned down The Beatles, chat at a talent contest. George recommends that Dick go to the Crawdaddy to watch the Rollin' Stones at their residency. He takes his advice and later signs the band to Decca.

Friends – It's 10 September 1963, and Andrew Loog Oldham is despondent. The Rolling Stones' first single, a cover of Chuck Berry's 'Come On', was released in July and its highest chart position was twenty-one. The band are in the studio trying to record a second single and it's not going well. Oldham takes a walk, and, as luck would have it, bumps into John and Paul. They say they've just written a new song. Oldham brings them back to the studio where the Rolling Stones watch them finish off the middle-eight within minutes at a table in the corner. The song is 'I Wanna Be Your Man'. The Stones' second single reaches number 12 in the UK charts. Inspired by watching John and Paul work, Oldham persuades Mick and Keith to start writing songs together.

Rivals – When Oldham first signs up the Rolling Stones he copies Brian Epstein's playbook with The Beatles, putting them in suits and commissioning smart, smiling photographs. However, he quickly realises that marketing the band as the anti-Beatles will be more effective and the headline 'Would You Let Your Sister Go With A Rolling Stone?' adorns a feature in *Melody Maker*. Keith is asked if they want to appeal to parents as well as teenagers. He replies: 'We don't particularly care . . . If they like us, good. If they don't, hard luck. We don't mind.' The band listen to 'Can't Buy Me Love', and Mick says of the song, 'It's something you can remember, but we won't remember it in years to come, like some of the other John and Paul things.' Their rebellious attitude is further enhanced by an appearance on *Juke Box Jury* where they rubbish every song, and in July 1965 when Jagger, Jones and

Wyman are each fined a fiver for 'insulting behaviour' – urinating on a garage wall in Forrest Gate. (Charlie Watts sat quietly in the car reading his evening newspaper.)

Friends – As the Rolling Stones' fame grows, both bands consult each other on their single and album release dates so there is no chance of a clash in vying for the number one spot.

Rivals – 1 May 1966, and for the first time both The Beatles and the Rolling Stones are booked to appear at the annual *NME* Poll Winners' Party. Oldham agrees in writing that the Rolling Stones will not appear just before The Beatles, making them look second fiddle. Instead, it's agreed that after the Stones' performance, the awards will be handed out, then The Beatles will perform. On the night, The Beatles arrive early as the Stones are playing. John insists that The Beatles go on stage as soon as the Stones come off. The Beatles are told to come back later and John explodes with anger, demanding that The Beatles go on stage right away or not at all. The *NME* stick to the agreement with Oldham, and The Beatles perform after the ceremony. The Beatles never play for the *NME* again.

Friends – When Mick is found guilty of possession of four pep pills and Keith of allowing drug taking in his home after the infamous Redlands bust of February 1967, it looks as if both of them will face jail time. *Times* editor William Rees-Mogg feels the court decision is unduly harsh and writes his famous 'Who breaks a butterfly on a wheel?' editorial, resulting in Keith's verdict being overturned and Mick being given a year's conditional discharge. To thank the fans for their support, the Stones record 'We Love You'. John and Paul come to the studio and help the band to arrange the song and provide backing vocals. In turn, Mick, Keith and Brian appear on various Beatles records, including 'Yellow Submarine' and 'All You Need Is Love'.

Friends – In another show of solidarity, The Beatles include a Shirley Temple doll wearing a stripey jumper that says 'Welcome The Rolling Stones' on the cover of *Sgt. Pepper*. The Stones reply on the cover of their 1967 psychedelic album *Their Satanic Majesties Request* – also designed by Peter Blake and photographed by Michael Cooper – with four Beatle-faced flowers.

Rivals – At the Vesuvio Club in early August 1968, a party is thrown for Mick Jagger's birthday and the launch of the band's new album *Beggars Banquet*. The album is well received. Paul arrives at the party with an acetate of the newly recorded Beatles' single 'Hey Jude'. He asks the DJ to play it, and the song goes down so well with the revellers that the DJ plays it over and over again. Mick is unhappy that his thunder has been stolen.

Rivals – In John's famously angry interview with Jann Wenner in *Rolling Stone* magazine, given after The Beatles had broken up, he lets loose a tirade against the Stones, saying, 'I resent the implication that the Stones are like revolutionaries and The Beatles weren't, you know? . . . They're not in the same class, music-wise or power-wise. Never were. And Mick always resented it. I never said anything, I always admired them because I like their funky music and I like their style . . . I like rock and roll and the direction they took after they got over trying to imitate us.'

95

THE SONGS THE BEATLES GAVE AWAY

Lennon-McCartney and Harrison didn't just keep The Beatles in songs. Often, they wrote songs for their fellow musicians. Here are the songs released in the UK that The Beatles gave away.

Fellow Liverpool bands and NEMS stablemates were the first beneficiaries.

Billy J. Kramer and the Dakotas
'I'll Be On My Way' (Lennon-McCartney)
Release date: April 1963
Highest chart position: 2
'I'll Be On My Way' was the B-side to 'Do You Want To Know A Secret', another Lennon-McCartney song, though The Beatles did their own version on *Please Please Me*.

'Bad To Me' (Lennon-McCartney)
Release date: June 1963
Highest chart position: 1
Again, the B-side was another Lennon-McCartney song, 'I Call Your Name', though The Beatles did their own version, found on the *Long Tall Sally* EP and later the *Past Masters One* compilation.

'I'll Keep You Satisfied' (Lennon-McCartney)
Release date: November 1963
Highest chart position: 4

'From A Window' (Lennon-McCartney)
Release date: July 1964
Highest chart position: 10

Tommy Quickly
'Tip Of My Tongue' (Lennon-McCartney)
Release date: August 1963
Didn't chart

The Fourmost
'Hello Little Girl' (Lennon-McCartney)
Release date: August 1963
Highest chart position: 9

'I'm In Love'
Release date: November 1963
Highest chart position: 17

Cilla Black
'Love Of The Loved' (Lennon-McCartney)
Release date: September 1963
Highest chart position: 35

'It's For You' (Lennon-McCartney)
Release date: July 1964
Highest chart position: 7

'Step Inside Love' (Lennon-McCartney)
Release date: March 1968
Highest chart position: 8

Beyond Merseybeat, Peter and Gordon – starring Jane Asher's brother, Peter – took on the most Lennon-McCartney originals.

Peter and Gordon
'A World Without Love' (Lennon-McCartney)
Release date: February 1964
Highest chart position: 1

'Nobody I Know' (Lennon-McCartney)
Release date: May 1964
Highest chart position: 10

'I Don't Want To See You Again' (Lennon-McCartney)
Release date: September 1964
Didn't chart

'Woman' (Lennon-McCartney)
Release date: February 1966
Highest chart position: 28
'Woman' was written by Paul using the pseudonym 'Bernard Webb' as an experiment to see how well a song he had written would do without his name attached. It also reached number fourteen in the US and number one in Canada.

And there's more . . .

Rolling Stones
'I Wanna Be Your Man' (Lennon-McCartney)
Release date: November 1963
Highest chart position: 12
The song was given to the Stones before The Beatles did their own version on *With The Beatles*.

The Strangers with Mike Shannon
'One And One Is Two' (Lennon-McCartney)
Release date: May 1964
Didn't chart

The Applejacks
'Like Dreamers Do' (Lennon-McCartney)
Release date: June 1964
Highest chart position: 20

P. J. Proby
'That Means A Lot' (Lennon-McCartney)
Release date: March 1965
Highest chart position: 30

The Chris Barber Band
'Catcall' (originally called 'Catswalk') (Lennon-McCartney)
Release date: July 1967
Didn't chart

The Black Dyke Mills Band
'Thingumybob' (Lennon-McCartney)
Release date: August 1968
Didn't chart

Jackie Lomax
'Sour Milk Sea' (Harrison)
Release date: August 1968
Didn't chart

Mary Hopkin
'Goodbye' (Lennon-McCartney)
Release date: March 1969
Highest chart position: 2

Badfinger
'Come And Get It' (McCartney)
Release date: December 1969
Highest chart position: 4

96

BEATLES COVER VERSIONS

Cover versions of The Beatles' work number in their thousands, and deserve a whole book to cover comprehensively. Here are some favourites – notable, surprising and plain bizarre.

'Misery' Kenny Lynch
The very first cover version to be released, in March 1963. Despite guitar performances by the legendary Bert Weedon and Joe Brown, it unfortunately didn't chart. There were no hard feelings on Kenny's part, though, as he later appeared in the gang of convicts on the cover of Paul McCartney and Wings album *Band On The Run*, alongside Michael Parkinson, James Coburn, Clement Freud, John Conteh and Christopher Lee.

'A Hard Day's Night' Peter Sellers
The pioneer of the comedy Beatles cover, Peter Sellers squeezes as much pathos as possible into the song as he channels Laurence Olivier as Richard III. Others followed, some funny only by accident: Pinky and Perky ('All My Loving'), Tiny Tim ('Nowhere Man'), Bill Cosby ('Sgt. Pepper's Lonely Hearts Club Band'), Telly Savalas ('Something'), Sean Connery ('In My Life'), Frankie Howerd ('Mean Mr Mustard') and Billy Connolly ('Being For The Benefit Of Mr. Kite!'). William Shatner boldly took 'Lucy In The Sky With Diamonds' . . . somewhere, Frank Sidebottom

interpreted a number of Beatles songs in his own imitable way, and Jim Carrey chewed the scenery performing 'I Am The Walrus' on George Martin's album *In My Life*.

'We Can Work It Out' Stevie Wonder
Many great funk and soul superstars brought their own style to Beatles classics, but Stevie Wonder's version of 'We Can Work It Out' might possibly be my favourite. An air of melancholy lingers in the original, but Stevie's version is a blast of pure joy, energy and vocal brilliance that transforms the song from a nervy lover's plea to a celebration of humanity. Other energetic soul covers include Otis Redding's 'Day Tripper', Earth, Wind and Fire's 'Got To Get You Into My Life', James Brown's 'Something', Bobby McFerrin's 'Drive My Car' and 'Get Back' by Ike & Tina Turner, with a special mention for Booker T. and the M.G.s' album, *McLemore Avenue*, the entire thing a funktastic tribute to *Abbey Road*.

'With A Little Help From My Friends' Joe Cocker
A cover that divides music fans: is it overblown or a powerhouse reimagining? I personally prefer the original. It's the perfect song for Ringo to sing to us all: personal, intimate and with a real faith in its sentiment. But there's no denying Joe Cocker takes the song into a different realm, a place where his salvation comes not from those around him, but from somewhere beyond. And for those who adore taking The Beatles to church, we mustn't forget Wilson Pickett's (and guitarist Duane Allman's) wonderful 'Hey Jude', Ray Charles's 'Eleanor Rigby', Marvin Gaye's 'Yesterday' and Aretha Franklin's 'Let It Be'.

'You Can't Do That' Nilsson
In his 1967 debut album *Pandemonium Shadow Show*, Harry

Nilsson packs in as many Beatles lyrics and references as possible in another of my favourite covers. Clearly a massive fan, it's a clever celebration of The Beatles' early work, and addictive listening. It's claimed that John, after receiving the album from Derek Taylor, listened to it for thirty-six hours straight. John later went on to become great friends with Nilsson, producing his album *Pussy Cats*. After John's death, Nilsson campaigned for gun control and donated his performance royalties to the Coalition to Stop Gun Violence.

'Something' Shirley Bassey

I knew this song as Bassey's before I knew it as a Beatles song, having watched her perform it on *Sunday Night at the London Palladium* as a youngster, and then impersonated by cabaret performer Joe Longthorne. The song, arranged with much beauty and a little funk, with vocals both sultry and dramatic, signalled a comeback for Bassey, who had fallen out of favour in the late sixties. Released in 1970, it was her biggest hit for years, reaching number four and spending twenty-two weeks in the UK charts, putting the girl from Tiger Bay firmly back in place as one of the country's top singers and performers.

'A Day In The Life' Wes Montgomery

Jazz guitarist Wes Montgomery dispenses with the original's existential exploration in this lush, chilled-out jazz instrumental that evokes cocktails in the garden and bare feet on the grass. Other Beatles jazz versions worth turning up are Ella Fitzgerald's stomping gem, 'Can't Buy Me Love', Peggy Lee's 'A Hard Day's Night', Sarah Vaughan's 'I Want You (She's So Heavy)', Buddy Rich's 'Norwegian Wood (This Bird Has Flown)' and Sammy Davis Jr's Beatles medley from his *Hearin' Is Believin'* album.

'I Want To Hold Your Hand' Sparks
Recorded while the band were experimenting with a more West Coast sound as they made the album *Big Beat*, the song was released as a single but didn't chart. It's a romantic, lush arrangement courtesy of the iconic Philadelphia MFSB team, and is complemented perfectly by Russell Mael's delicate vocals. It's a mystery to me why this version is not better known.

'Tomorrow Never Knows' 801
Why would anyone attempt to cover 'Tomorrow Never Knows'? As if anyone could better the original! Making a decent fist of it, though, is Brian Eno, who, in 1976, teamed up with his former Roxy Music bandmate Phil Manzanera, as well as Bill MacCormick, Francis Monkman, Simon Phillips and Lloyd Watson to perform three concerts as 801. There is some suitably funky bass and guitar to make this version worth a listen.

'Ticket To Ride' Hüsker Dü
John Lennon always liked how 'heavy' the original was, so it was only right that hardcore punk rockers Hüsker Dü reply to that observation with a version even heavier and fuzzier, turning up the guitars and using the 'Tomorrow Never Knows' drum pattern. Still, heavier to me is The Carpenters' lush arrangement, Karen Carpenter's melancholy timbre embodying heartbreak and loneliness.

'Norwegian Wood (This Bird Has Flown)' Cornershop
The closing track on their 1997 bestselling album *When I Was Born For The 7th Time*, Cornershop's version sticks fairly close to the original musically but instead translates the lyrics into Punjabi, a playful nod to The Beatles 'introducing' Eastern music to Western audiences.

'Within You Without You' Anthony Newley

Of all the Beatles covers I have heard so far, this ranks as the weirdest. Recorded as part of a 1977 TV special called *The Beatles Forever*, Newley's heavy vibrato and cockney accent clashes with the clunking Indian soundscape, making him sound like a strange pantomime ghost.

The Grey Album Danger Mouse

Not strictly a cover version, but this piece of work from 2004 merits attention for its imagination and virtuosity. Using The Beatles' White Album and an a capella version of Jay-Z's *Black Album*, Danger Mouse mashes Jay-Z's rhymes with samples of Beatles arrangements to amazing effect. Unfortunately, the buzz around the album reached the ears of EMI who asked Danger Mouse to halt distribution despite approval by Ringo and Paul. Paul was more sanguine than the record company, saying of their reaction, 'Take it easy, guys. It's a tribute.' In protest, online activists organised Grey Tuesday where websites offered *The Grey Album* as a free download for a twenty-four-hour period. Over 100,000 copies were downloaded.

'Octopus's Garden' The Muppets

Sung by Robin the Frog, along with Kermit and spirited backing vocals from mermaid Miss Piggy, amidst some friendly clams and goldfish, it's as perfectly enchanting as it sounds. The Muppets have covered many Beatles songs, most recently, in June 2020 in lockdown, 'With A Little Help From My Friends' alongside chat show host James Corden.

97

SOLO WORK

Everything will be okay in the end. If it's not okay, it's not the end.
— John Lennon

John started on his solo career before The Beatles had even split. Alongside Yoko, the couple collaborated on avant-garde releases, art projects and peace activism. In 1970, they embarked on Primal Scream therapy with founder Arthur Janov, inspiring the songs that made up John's first commercial solo album *John Lennon/ Plastic Ono Band*. The songs were musically spare and lyrically raw: John was making it clear he had moved on from his old band, declaring in 'God' 'I don't believe in Beatles'. The title song of his next album, *Imagine*, was his most iconic release, and he continued to quash the hope that The Beatles would get back together with the song, 'How Do You Sleep?', a savage yet funky attack on his old songwriting partner. In 1971, John and Yoko moved to New York and continued supporting causes such as Irish republicanism, civil rights and the political activism of John Sinclair. Unfortunately, this work and his conviction for drug possession were to have an impact on John being awarded US citizenship – the Nixon administration tried to get him deported and the FBI opened a file on him – and he spent much of his time in the early seventies battling with immigration authorities. He was finally awarded his Green Card in 1975.

John and Yoko split up in 1973, and he went to Los Angeles

John and Yoko with David Bowie, Simon and Garfunkel and
Roberta Flack at the 17th Annual Grammy Awards, 1975. *Alamy*

with their personal assistant, now his lover, May Pang, to continue
working on his music, while carousing with his showbiz friends.
He later referred to this time apart from Yoko as his 'lost weekend',
though their separation lasted for eighteen months. His musical
career suffered during this period too, with his albums *Some Time
In New York City*, *Mind Games*, *Walls And Bridges* and *Rock 'n'
Roll* having mixed chart success. John collaborated with many
musicians throughout the seventies including Harry Nilsson,
Mick Jagger, Ringo Starr and, most successfully, David Bowie, on
'Fame', and Elton John. Elton's 'Whatever Gets You Through the
Night' was a US number one.

Reunited with Yoko, in 1975 they had a baby boy, Sean, and
John became a house husband, looking after his son, baking bread,
travelling and sailing, until he decided to record music again in

1980. The album, *Double Fantasy*, was released in November, and was performing decently when he was shot and killed outside his home by Mark David Chapman. In the weeks following his death, *Double Fantasy* topped the charts in both the UK and the US.

Since his death, John Lennon's life and work garners new fans with each generation, and his legacy as one of the most talented songwriters of the 20th century remains. He is still fascinating to writers, musicians, artists and filmmakers, both as a flawed, complicated, contradictory man and as a cultural icon.

> *We were a boy band. It's not a bad thing but*
> *after a while you felt like you wanted to move on.*
> – Paul McCartney

Paul has enjoyed a rich and varied music career since The Beatles split up, indulging his curiosity and creative impulses, and becoming the most successful (and one of the wealthiest) musicians on the planet. After releasing two critically panned solo albums, *McCartney* and *Ram* (both now widely reappraised as brilliant), Paul started a new band, Wings, with the core of Linda, Denny Laine and himself, and an ever-changing roster of guitarists and drummers. With a back-to-basics approach, they launched their career by touring the UK, playing to university crowds and taking money on the door. In 1973, Paul found himself back at the top of the charts with a number one single, 'My Love', in the US, then a Top 10 hit on both sides of the Atlantic with his Bond theme, 'Live And Let Die', which was also nominated for an Academy Award. Paul, Linda and Denny then travelled to Lagos, Nigeria, to record *Band On The Run*, the album that cemented Wings' international success. Back in the big time, Wings toured the world, playing stadiums and arenas, and continued to release hit albums and singles, including *Venus And Mars*, *Wings At The Speed Of Sound*, 'Silly Love Songs', 'Let 'Em In', and 'Mull Of Kintyre', a Scottish folk waltz, which, at the height of punk, overtook The Beatles' 'She Loves You' as the bestselling single of all time.

The interpersonal relationships in Wings were often volatile, and, in 1980, Wings broke up. Paul continued to enjoy chart success as a solo artist, particularly with albums *McCartney II*, *Tug Of War* and *Pipes Of Peace*, and his collaborations with Stevie Wonder, 'Ebony And Ivory', and Michael Jackson, 'The Girl Is Mine' and 'Say, Say, Say'. After the commercial success but critical reception of the children's song 'We All Stand Together', no single of his would reach the Top 10 in the UK until 2015 and the unprecedented talent mash-up, 'FourFiveSeconds', a

Paul and Linda backstage during the Wings 1973 UK tour. *Alamy*

collaboration with Rihanna and Kanye West. Kanye memorably described the experience: 'I'm just saying I'm angst, a bit like John Lennon. And the tension creates a new magic, the pressure creates the diamonds from the coal, and he [Paul] came with the best vibes ever.'

As an albums artist, however, his fans more often than not would ensure that they would reach the Top 10. Paul carries on making music regardless, with his last album, *Egypt Station* (2018), receiving critical acclaim – *NME* praised it as an 'album of upbeat and winsome notes . . . simple and honest, as if one of the most famous people in the world has left his diary open for us to read' – and reaching number one in the US and number three in the UK.

Although Paul famously does not own the publishing rights to the Lennon-McCartney songbook, other than 'Love Me Do' and 'P.S. I Love You', which he procured from Ardmore & Beechwood in 1978, his company, MPL, has acquired a great number of assets, including the publishing rights to musicals *Annie*, *Guys and Dolls* and *Grease*, as well as the Buddy Holly catalogue.

To try to fit Paul's post-Beatles achievements into a few paragraphs obviously cannot do justice to his creativity. With his boundless, restless imagination, side projects have included forays into classical music, electronica, film, painting, poetry and children's books. He is also a vocal campaigner for the environment, animal rights and vegetarianism, and co-founder and patron of the Liverpool Institute of Performing Arts. He was awarded a knighthood in 1997, but wears his legendary status and his many accolades lightly as he continues to travel the world playing to record-breaking audiences. He's clearly having far too much fun to ever consider stopping.

The Beatles saved the world from boredom.
— George Harrison

They say it's the quiet ones you've got to watch. George's solo career got off to a flyer in 1970 with the release of the majestic triple album *All Things Must Pass*, packed with songs he had been writing in the last years of his time with The Beatles. The album was a hit worldwide, and the beautiful 'My Sweet Lord' topped the charts on both sides of the Atlantic. He cemented his stature in 1971 with the Concert for Bangladesh, organised with Ravi Shankar. Pre-empting Live Aid, the event pioneered the charity musical event and, despite frustrating tax complications that dragged on for years, by 1985 had raised around $12 million for refugees in the war-torn region. Alongside friends Eric Clapton, Bob Dylan, Badfinger, Billy Preston and Ringo Starr, George played two sell-out shows in New York's Madison Square Garden, which were later recorded and released as a Grammy award-winning album.

Although he enjoyed playing and had developed his own distinctive slide-guitar sound, George was always a reluctant pop star. He disliked the caprices of the industry as well as the compromises and promotional grind it takes to build momentum for a sustained musical career. He didn't receive the same kind of commercial success for each successive album release throughout the seventies, and a 1974 US tour carried out when his voice was croaky and shot from drink and drug excess was a low point. Critics scathingly described it as The Dark Hoarse Tour. He came close to a breakdown, and his inner conflict between his spiritual quest and the easy access to decadence and materialism troubled him, as did the copyright infringement ruling that found him guilty of 'subconscious' plagiarism of The Chiffons' hit, 'He's So Fine'. George claimed that the inspiration for 'My Sweet Lord'

George and Ravi Shankar promote *The Concert for Bangladesh* in New York. *Alamy*

had in fact come from 'Oh, Happy Day' by the Edwin Hawkins Singers, but the subsequent legal disputes dragged on for years and took a toll on his confidence as a songwriter.

George's second marriage to Olivia Arias and the birth of his son, Dhani, in 1978, heralded a step back from the spotlight and allowed him to indulge in his many other interests: gardening in the grounds of his Friar Park estate, a renewed attention to his spiritual practice, his love for racing cars and Formula 1, his humanitarian efforts and in running HandMade Films. He started the film company with a friend of Peter Sellers, Denis O'Brien, when they decided to step in to rescue the production of the Monty Python team's second film, *Life of Brian*. George mortgaged his home, prompting Eric Idle to comment that it was the most anybody's ever paid for a cinema ticket in history.

HandMade would go on to produce a number of significant British films, including *The Long Good Friday*, *Time Bandits*, *A Private Function* and *Withnail and I*. Sadly, after a run of poor performances at the box office, the company ceased operating in 1991 and George sued his business partner for fraud and negligence. He was awarded $11.6 million in 1996.

In the late eighties, George experienced a critical and commercial revival with his *Cloud Nine* album, which spawned the Top 5 single 'Got My Mind Set On You', and with The Traveling Wilburys, which included his friends Bob Dylan, Jeff Lynne, Tom Petty and Roy Orbison. Frustratingly short-lived, due to the death of Orbison, the band were much loved, achieving a number one album, *Traveling Wilburys Vol. 1*.

Other than during the *Anthology* project, George shunned the spotlight in the last decade of his life, and his final album, *Brainwashed*, was released posthumously in 2002, having been completed by his son, Dhani, and Jeff Lynne.

He may not have liked being pushed to the front of the stage, but George's talent, good taste and generosity as a musician and a man will always be rightly celebrated. He showed that there are unexpected ways to be a superstar.

Everybody loves Ringo. Not just because he's a Beatle,
not just because he's one of the tastiest drummers ever,
but because he radiates that peace and love.
– David Lynch

Ringo started his solo career not thinking of huge chart success but to please his mum. In a move that would later be copied by many recording artists, in 1970 he released an album of standards called *Sentimental Journey*. The album didn't do too badly, getting into the UK Top 10. He then took a trip to Nashville to record (in three days) a country album, *Beacoups Of Blues*, which didn't trouble the charts but fulfilled a long-held ambition. Meanwhile, he was having huge success in the singles charts with 'It Don't Come Easy' and 'Back Off Boogaloo', which both became Top 10 hits in the UK and the US. The year 1973 was his most commercially successful, with the release of the album *Ringo*. It featured songs written by John, Paul and George, and spawned Top 10 singles in the UK and two number-one singles in the US with 'Photograph' and 'You're Sixteen'.

Ringo was never to enjoy big chart success again, but he continues to record, and play drums on other artists' albums – B.B. King, Peter Frampton, Carly Simon, Bob Dylan, Howlin' Wolf, Doris Troy, Carl Perkins and even Vera Lynn. He has also enjoyed a varied acting career, with mixed success, collaborating with many top actors and directors, including a star turn with David Essex in *That'll Be the Day*, playing the Pope in Ken Russell's *Lisztomania*, starring with Frank Zappa in *200 Motels*, appearing in Martin Scorsese's documentary on The Band, *The Last Waltz*, and meeting his second wife, Barbara Bach, on the prehistoric comedy *Caveman*. He also directed and starred in the T. Rex documentary *Born to Boogie* and narrated the children's TV series *Thomas the Tank Engine* in both the UK and the US.

After The Beatles split up, Ringo, ever the bon viveur, jetted round the world having fun with his many showbiz pals, but by the mid-eighties his heavy drink and drug habit (16 bottles of wine and a pile of coke a day at one point, he confessed) was taking a toll. He was experiencing blackouts and narrowly escaped being seriously hurt in a car crash. He and Barbara decided to attend an addiction clinic in 1988, and he has been sober since then,

Ringo and David Essex in *That'll Be The Day*. Alamy

attributing his remarkably youthful appearance to 'just working out and eating carrots'. He replaced his partying with touring and established his All-Starr band with an ever-changing line up of musician friends such as Joe Walsh, Dave Edmunds, Todd Rundgren, Billy Preston, John Entwistle and many more. Along with his renewed interest in transcendental meditation – he is a regular fundraiser for the David Lynch Foundation – and a switch to a vegetarian diet, Ringo is still living life to the fullest. He splits his time between the UK and the US, and was appointed a Knight Bachelor in 2018. He celebrated his milestone eightieth birthday under COVID-19 lockdown in July 2020 by creating a livestreamed video montage of messages and performances from his musician friends, including Paul McCartney and Joe Walsh, as well as members of his family, while raising a ton of money for charity.

98

THE DEATH OF JOHN LENNON:
08/12/80

If everyone demanded peace instead of another
television set, then there'd be peace.
– John Lennon

Mark David Chapman was born in May 1955 in Forth Worth, Texas, to a nurse mother and Air Force sergeant father. His father was a domineering presence, and Chapman was often bullied at school. He sought solace in the music of The Beatles and in creating an imaginary world where he oversaw the 'little people'.

Leaving school, he became a born-again Christian and worked with vulnerable children at a Georgia YMCA. Later, he helped refugees from Vietnam and Lebanon. His mental health came under question when he dropped out of college and moved to Hawaii where he attempted suicide. On release from hospital, he worked first as a printer then as a security guard. He travelled around Asia, the Middle East and Europe, and married his travel agent Gloria Abe, but his obsession with John began to dominate his thoughts.

Reading of Lennon's wealth, Chapman became fixated on the idea that John had abandoned his ideals. This, together with relating to *The Catcher in the Rye*'s Holden Caulfield's disdain for 'phoneys', convinced him that Lennon's death would be justified vengeance.

He flew into New York in December 1980 with a rucksack full of Beatles music and a copy of *The Catcher in the Rye*, on which he inscribed 'This is my statement'. He bought a copy of *Double Fantasy* and *Playboy* magazine, which featured a lengthy interview with John, and over the weekend of 6–7 December he hung around the Dakota building waiting for his chance.

On 8 December, John started the day with breakfast at his favourite restaurant, La Fortuna, before getting a haircut in a fifties Teddy boy style for his photography session with Annie Leibovitz later in the day. He was interviewed by RKO Radio in his apartment, and, after Leibovitz had left, he and Yoko went to the Record Plant to continue work on Yoko's song 'Walking On Thin Ice'. Before getting into his car, John signed Chapman's new copy of *Double Fantasy*.

In the studio, during a break from work, John phoned his aunt Mimi. When they had finished work for the evening, Yoko suggested going out to dinner, but John preferred to go home to say good night to Sean at bedtime.

Arriving back at the Dakota, John and Yoko left their limousine and walked towards the door. Chapman was waiting. He pulled out a .38 revolver and fired five shots at John's back. John collapsed to the ground, while Yoko screamed for help. The Dakota's porter called the police and covered John with his coat. Chapman stayed on the scene, taking out his copy of *The Catcher in the Rye* to read until the police arrived. He was arrested without incident, and John was rushed to the Roosevelt Hospital where he was taken into the emergency room, but it was too late. He was declared dead at 11.07 p.m.

It has never really been clear why Chapman killed John Lennon. He adored The Beatles as a teenager and idolised John especially, and had no criminal convictions. He remains in the

Wende Correctional Facility in Alden, New York, to this day, having been denied parole ten times, and claims to think about John signing his album every day.

Fans gather in Central Park, New York, to pay tribute to John, December 1980. *Alamy*

99

THE BEATLES RE-FORM

As far as I'm concerned, there won't be a Beatles
reunion as long as John Lennon remains dead.
– George Harrison

The nineties was a good decade to be a Beatles fan. We could look forward to new releases in the way fans had done in the sixties.

First, in November 1994, The Beatles released the double *Live At The BBC* album. In the early years of Beatles stardom, they appeared on fifty-two BBC radio programmes, playing to an audience and chatting to broadcaster Brian Matthews. Some of these sessions had been bootlegged over the years, but the album, with fifty-six songs plus snippets of conversation and skits, was still highly anticipated. The album featured live versions of The Beatles' early classics, but also a swathe of rock 'n' roll and R&B numbers, highlighting the breadth of the live repertoire they had honed in Hamburg and Liverpool.

Live At The BBC topped the UK charts on its release, reached number three in the US Hot 100, and sold eight million copies worldwide in its first year of release. In the UK, a single, 'Baby It's You', was released in April 1995 and reached number seven in the charts.

Appetite whetted, Apple then announced the *Anthology* project, something that had been tempting in-the-know Beatles fans for decades, as rumours of Aspinall's documentary *The Long and Winding Road* had routinely surfaced since the early seventies. Now, the project, renamed, had been green lit, with each surviving Beatle taking part in interviews and offering footage from their personal archives, and Yoko gave her permission for the Lennons' archive to be searched so that John's voice would be heard throughout too.

As well as the documentary, Derek Taylor was drafted in to pull together archive quotes to be used in a book, and George Martin joined the project to oversee the assembly of three double albums of unreleased songs and outtakes.

In the meantime, Paul, George and Ringo were contemplating getting together to record instrumental incidental music for the documentary. Then came the news everyone wanted to hear: The Beatles were re-forming.

Since the official split in 1970, the question of The Beatles getting back together again was a constant in media interviews, with million-dollar offers following them throughout their solo careers. After John's death, the clamour quietened, although the suggestion of one of John's sons, Julian or Sean, taking his place was a frequent suggestion.

Now, with a gift from Yoko of three unreleased demos of John's – 'Free As A Bird', 'Real Love' and 'Now And Then', it was possible for the four to be reunited, virtually, in the studio. At George's suggestion, Jeff Lynne was called in to produce, and The Beatles worked on the songs in both Paul and George's home studios.

With the documentary nearing completion, the television rights were sold to ABC in the US, and to ITV in the UK for £5 million. Shown in six parts in the UK between 26 November and 31 December 1995, and in three parts in the US between 19 and 23 November, the documentary concluded with the premiere of the video for the new Beatles single 'Free As A Bird'. Directed by Joe Pytka, the video is a bird's-eye view of a world full of Beatles references, filmed in many Liverpool locations.

'Free As A Bird' was released in the UK on 4 December 1995. It missed out on the coveted Christmas number one spot, kept off the top of the charts by Michael Jackson's 'Earth Song'. However, the song won two Grammy awards, one for the Best Pop Performance by a Duo or Group with Vocal and the other for Best Short Form Music Video.

The first Beatles *Anthology* album was released in November 1995, and was once again kept off the top spot in the UK charts (this time by Robson & Jerome). It hit the top spot in the US, as did the second and third *Anthology* albums. In the UK, *Anthology 2* topped the chart, and *Anthology 3* reached number four.

The *Anthology* book topped the bestseller lists in both the UK and US, and the extended documentary was released as a video, laser disc and then DVD box set.

'Real Love', the second single from the re-formed Beatles, was released in March 1996 and reached number four in the UK chart, with Radio 1 controversially withholding it from their playlist, having decided that the status of The Beatles was only of interest to older listeners. The third song, 'Now And Then', was never released, as George was unsatisfied with the result.

100

THE DEATH OF GEORGE HARRISON: 29/11/01

There is no such thing as death, only in the physical sense.
— George Harrison

In the summer of 1997, George discovered a lump on his neck. He underwent an operation to remove the malignant tumour as well as radiation therapy. He acknowledged that his tobacco habit was the cause (George was an enthusiastic smoker from an early age, who could get through three or four packs a day), admitting that he had taken up smoking again after a period of abstinence.

In better health, on 30 December 1999, he and Olivia were woken up in the middle of the night by the sound of breaking glass. George went to investigate while Olivia phoned the emergency services. He came upon a young man, Mick Abram, who attacked George with a kitchen knife, stabbing him multiple times and puncturing a lung. Olivia managed to save her husband by knocking out Abram with a heavy brass lamp. George was rushed to hospital where he underwent surgery to remove part of his lung. In public he downplayed the incident, but it affected him deeply.

In March 2001, George's cancer returned and another tumour was removed from his lung. He travelled to Bellinzona, Switzerland, to recover under the care of the Oncology Institute of Southern Switzerland, staying in a nearby lakeside lodge on the Italian border.

By late October, he discovered that the cancer had spread from his lungs to his brain, and he flew to Staten Island in the US to undergo experimental radiation treatment. Unhappy with the care he was receiving, he then travelled to Los Angeles for more radiotherapy.

George's spiritual beliefs meant that he didn't fear death; he was adamant that he would leave his body in a state of Krishna consciousness. He died in Paul's Beverly Hills property on 29 November 2001 at 1.30 p.m. surrounded by Olivia, son Dhani and a group of Krishna devotees who chanted as he passed. Later, his family travelled to Varanasi to cast his ashes into the River Ganges.

In January 2002, 'My Sweet Lord' topped the UK charts for the second time.

101

THE BEATLES IN THE DIGITAL AGE

My model for business is The Beatles: they were four guys that kept each others' negative tendencies in check; they balanced each other. And the total was greater than the sum of the parts.
– Steve Jobs

Neil Aspinall guided Apple business with dedication and doggedness until his retirement in 2007. With the ethos that The Beatles' musical legacy should not be undervalued, their music was notable for its absence when the iTunes store opened for business in January 2001.

The Beatles and Apple's relationship with Steve Jobs' company had been contentious since 1978 when Aspinall discovered the existence of the fledgling computing firm using their trademarked name and strikingly similar logo. An agreement that Jobs could retain the name and logo was settled between them – as long as Apple Computers stayed away from the music business. As Jobs' company grew and diversified, it found itself in court up against The Beatles on countless occasions. Just before his retirement, Aspinall had reached an out-of-court settlement with Jobs over the iPod and iTunes store.

Yet it wasn't until 16 November 2010 that it was announced that The Beatles' back catalogue would be available to download from the iTunes store in a deal that surpassed standard royalty rates for downloads. For a year, iTunes would have exclusive rights to The

Beatles' digital content, with each album also offering additional digital content such as lyrics, photographs and artworks. And for $149 customers could download the entire back catalogue with exclusive access to the video of The Beatles' first concert in the Washington Coliseum way back in 1964.

Within twenty-four hours of being launched, fifteen per cent of the iTunes Top 200 singles chart was made up of Beatles songs, going up to twenty-five per cent within forty-eight hours. In the album chart, both the *Red* and *Blue* greatest hits albums had hit the Top 20 along with *Sgt. Pepper's Lonely Hearts Club Band*, while ten more albums featured in the Top 75. By the end of the first week, there had been two million Beatles downloads.

The Beatles, understandably reluctant to devalue their music, were also late to the streaming party. They finally announced their availability to streaming platforms on Christmas Eve, 2015. In a year, The Beatles had achieved a jaw-dropping 2 billion streams, with 'Come Together' the most popular. By 2020, The Beatles Top 10 streams were:

1.   Here Comes The Sun
2.   Let It Be
3.   Hey Jude
4.   Come Together
5.   Twist And Shout
6.   Help!
7.   Blackbird
8.   In My Life
9.   Yesterday
10. All You Need Is Love

Figures also showed that the biggest age demographic for these streams was 18–24, indicating that The Beatles continue to gather fans with each new generation. On YouTube too, The Beatles statistics are staggering, with over 1.5 trillion views and a daily average viewing figure of 1.5 million. By 2020, the top ten most viewed videos were:

1. Don't Let Me Down
2. Hey Jude
3. Hello, Goodbye
4. A Day In The Life
5. We Can Work It Out
6. Penny Lane
7. Help!
8. Revolution
9. Come Together
10. Yellow Submarine

The world, it seems, will never tire of those four lads from Liverpool who took on the world and won.

A giant iTunes poster of The Beatles adorns HMV Apollo, London. *Alamy*

BEATLEY STUFF

I've read a lot of Beatles books since I was a teenager, and all of them have helped in the writing of this guide. Should you want to dive deeper into the Beatles story and feed your growing Beatlemania, here are some recommendations to get you started.

The Beatles, *The Beatles Anthology* (Chronicle Books, 2012)

Michael Braun, *Love Me Do!: The Beatles' Progress* (Graymalkin Media, 2019)

Alan Clayson, *Ringo Starr* (Sanctuary Publishing, 2001)

Hunter Davies, *The Beatles Book* (Ebury Press, 2019)

Richard DiLello, *The Longest Cocktail Party: An Insider Account of The Beatles & the Wild Rise and Fall of Their Multi-Million Dollar Apple Empire* (Alfred Publishing, 2014)

Peter Doggett, *You Never Give Me Your Money: The Battle for the Soul of The Beatles* (Vintage, 2010)

Tom Doyle, *Man on the Run: Paul McCartney in the 1970s* (Polygon, 2014)

Cynthia Lennon, *John* (Hodder Paperbacks, 2006)

John Lennon, *A Spaniard in the Works* (Canongate, 2014)

John Lennon, *In His Own Write* (Canongate, 2014)

Mark Lewisohn, *The Beatles: All These Years Volume 1: Tune In* (Little, Brown, 2015)

Mark Lewisohn, *The Complete Beatles Chronicle* (Hamlyn, 2000)

Ian MacDonald, *Revolution in the Head: The Beatles' Records and the Sixties* (Vintage, 2008)

John McMillian, *Beatles vs. Stones* (Simon & Schuster, 2014)

Ken McNab, *And in the End: The Last Days of The Beatles* (Polygon, 2019) Barry Miles, *Paul McCartney: Many Years from Now* (Vintage, 1998)

Philip Norman, *John Lennon: The Life* (HarperCollins, 2009)

Philip Norman, *Paul McCartney: The Biography* (Weidenfeld & Nicolson, 2017)

Philip Norman, *Shout! The True Story of The Beatles* (Pan, 2004)

Yoko Ono, *Grapefruit* (Simon & Schuster, 2000)

David Quantick, *Revolution: The Making of the Beatles White Album* (Spruce, 2002)

Derek Taylor, *As Time Goes By* (Faber & Faber, 2018)

Graeme Thomson, *George Harrison: Behind the Locked Door* (Omnibus, 2016)

Steve Turner, *Beatles '66: The Revolutionary Year* (Ecco, 2017)

Jann S. Wenner, *Lennon Remembers* (Verso, 2001)

I would also heartily recommend a trawl through the Beatles Bible website – www.beatlesbible.com – an amazing wealth of information and great stories. Also of great help in putting together this guide was www.rocksbackpages.com, an amazing archive of music reviews and features, and www.officialcharts.com for UK chart statistics.

ACKNOWLEDGEMENTS

Thank you John, Paul, George and Ringo.

Thanks to all the writers, film-makers, photographers, artists and musicians who have allowed my Beatlemania to flourish with all your Beatles-loving work.

Thanks to all my friends and family who have listened to me babble on about The Beatles over the years (sorry for ruining all our walks to and from school, Lisa!), and for those who sang along with me too (it's all your fault, Linda!), and who have encouraged me at various stages of writing.

Thanks especially to my sister, Jillian, who has been listening to all the podcasts, reading all the books, and watching all the YouTube videos along with me while I've been working on this. It was good to have a fellow fanatic along for the ride – you understand how important it is to know that George's hair was the best in 1966, and Paul's was the best in 1967.

Thanks to my publisher, Pete Burns, for your friendly perseverance in asking me to write *Beatles 101* in the first place, and for your easy-going encouragement throughout.

Thanks too to my editor, Alison Rae, for such an enjoyable collaboration. Is it always this much fun?

Thanks to Helen Mockridge, Jamie Harris and Lucy Mertekis for banging the *101* drum.

Finally, thank you, readers. I hope you have enjoyed the show.

POLARIS
PUBLISHING